Third Edition

English Language Learners

in Your Classroom

English Language Learners

Third Edition

in Your Classroom

Strategies
That
Work

**Ellen Kottler • Jeffrey A. Kottler
Chris Street**

CORWIN PRESS
A SAGE Company
Thousand Oaks, CA 91320

For information:

Corwin Press
A SAGE Company
2455 Teller Road
Thousand Oaks, California 91320
www.corwinpress.com

SAGE India Pvt. Ltd.
B 1/I 1 Mohan Cooperative
   Industrial Area
Mathura Road, New Delhi 110044
India

SAGE Ltd.
1 Oliver's Yard
55 City Road
London EC1Y 1SP
United Kingdom

SAGE Asia-Pacific Pte. Ltd.
33 Pekin Street #02–01
Far East Square
Singapore 048763

Printed in the United States of America

Library of Congress Cataloging-in-Publication Data

Kottler, Ellen.
English language learners in your classroom: Strategies that work / Ellen Kottler, Jeffrey A. Kottler, and Chris Street.—3rd ed.
     p. cm.
Rev. ed. of: Children with limited English. 2002.
Includes bibliographical references and index.
ISBN 978-1-4129-5816-5 (cloth)—ISBN 978-1-4129-5817-2 (pbk.)

   1. English language—Study and teaching—Foreign speakers. 2. Children of immigrants—Education. 3. Language and education. I. Kottler, Jeffrey A. II. Street, Chris. III. Kottler, Ellen. Children with limited English. IV. Title.
PE1128.A2K68 2008
428.0071—dc22   2007026280

This book is printed on acid-free paper.

07   08   09   10   11   10   9   8   7   6   5   4   3   2   1

Acquisitions Editor:	Rachel Livsey
Managing Editor:	Jessica Allan
Editorial Assistant:	Joanna Coelho
Production Editor:	Melanie Birdsall
Copy Editor:	Bill Bowers
Typesetter:	C&M Digitals (P) Ltd.
Proofreader:	Tracy Marcynzsyn
Indexer:	Judy Hunt
Cover Designer:	Lisa Miller

Contents

Preface

If there is one challenge that teachers are likely to continue facing in coming years, it will be working with an increasingly diverse student population. This will be true not only in terms of the cultural backgrounds of children, but also in terms of the languages they speak. Already in many schools, English is the native language for only a minority of the school population. During lunch, an astute observer can hear literally dozens of different languages being spoken in a single school. Needless to say, it makes for some very interesting work in the classroom when a significant number of students may not be able to communicate effectively with the teacher, or with one another, much less understand the dominant language of instruction.

As just one example, one of our students, Thuy, moved from Vietnam to Southern California when she was nine years old. She had been a confident and well-liked student back home, with lots of friends. Yet once she arrived at her new school in America, she found herself isolated and confused. She didn't understand any English, so she found it difficult to interact with any of the other students or communicate her interests to her teacher.

There was only one other Vietnamese student in Thuy's school, which was located in a predominately Mexican American part of the region, yet even this student wanted nothing to do with this foreigner; she didn't want to lose her own popularity by associating with the new kid who didn't talk. Over the coming days and weeks, Thuy tried hard to pick up the language of her new country, but it was difficult when everyone ignored her. She listened to conversations as much as possible and tried to practice pronouncing the strange, new words when she was alone. Eventually, through persistence and a level of desperation to communicate with her age-mates, Thuy was able to learn enough rudimentary grammar and vocabulary to begin carrying on basic conversations. Now she was making progress!

Imagine Thuy's surprise when she soon discovered that she had been learning Spanish, not English! Since Spanish was the primary language of the children in the school, that was the primary means by which they were talking to one another, and the language that Thuy found herself acquiring—all the time believing that she had been learning English. This is but one illustration of the language complexity that exists in so many of our schools today.

Whether students are recent immigrants, inhabitants of a bilingual (or trilingual) home, or living in homes in which only native languages are spoken, they struggle tremendously with the burdens of not only keeping up with their schoolwork and establishing a social network, but also doing so with limited or nonexistent English-speaking skills. Their school performance suffers significantly, or, as in the case of children like Thuy, they may become isolated and see themselves as worthless, stupid, or poor learners.

When such a student is first presented in the classroom doorway, many questions may come to the teacher's mind: How can I possibly help this student when we don't even speak the same language? How will the other students react to having this person in their midst? How can I meet this student's special needs and provide a successful school experience? What can I do to make the adjustment easiest for all of us? And, how can I do this without exhausting myself in the process?

This ever more frequent situation does indeed present some obstacles. Fortunately, there are a number of options available to the general education classroom teacher who is looking for supplemental skills, ideas, and resources to better serve students acquiring English. The purpose of this book is to help teachers function more effectively with this student population and to do so in a way that enhances rather than complicates the classroom environment.

WHO CAN USE THIS BOOK

This book is directed first to the population of beginning teachers who are being initiated into the realities of teaching as a career. It is overwhelming enough to think about managing a relatively homogeneous group of students without contemplating the added complexities of working with a class in which the children don't all speak the same language. Useful strategies for English language learners will thus augment a teacher's repertoire. Indeed, some school districts organize support groups for new teachers in which they can talk about issues and situations that confront them, such as working with English learners in the regular classroom. The strategies presented here will serve as a handy reference for teachers facing an increasingly diverse school population.

Next, students in teacher education courses will find this a useful primary or supplementary text. As teacher candidates prepare to meet the needs of diverse school populations, this book addresses the concerns and fears of those who have not had the training or opportunity to work with English learners.

Also, veteran teachers who are experiencing professional transitions in their work—who may have logged years of experience in the classroom but have had few opportunities to work with students new to the English language—will also find many of the concepts and methods described in this book quite helpful.

Finally, anyone involved in professional development for teachers, such as curriculum specialists, teacher mentors, and administrators, will find this book a valuable reference.

OVERVIEW OF CONTENTS

This book is derived from a previous work, *Children With Limited English: Teaching Strategies for the Regular Classroom*. When first published, it was one of the few resources available for practicing teachers. The second edition was expanded to include material on cultural backgrounds, values, learning styles, multiple intelligences, and applications of brain research to the practice of teaching diverse students. Since that time, there has been new thinking in the field, additional research, and many new teaching innovations that have been incorporated into contemporary practice. *English Language Learners in Your Classroom: Strategies That Work* greatly improves the previous book, with connections to current research, additional teaching strategies for building literacy, and the inclusion of checklists and tables, including how to create a comfortable classroom environment, develop a student roster of English learners, and use a guided lesson plan format.

Most significantly, we have added a new coauthor and voice to this project, that of Chris Street, who provides additional expertise in the areas of literacy, technology, and teacher preparation. New to this edition are updated demographic information with future projection trends; a separate chapter on literacy skills with specific resources for reading, writing, speaking, and listening activities; and a reinvigorated chapter on integrating current technology in the classroom, with suggestions for online resources.

The progression of chapters follows a pattern that resembles quite closely what practicing teachers actually do when they face the challenges of helping English learners. The first two chapters address the crucial task of developing relationships with students and parents in such a way as to build trust and establish a comfortable environment. Chapter 3 reviews principles related to second-language development. Chapters 4, 5, and 6 present a wealth of practical teaching strategies. Chapter 7 focuses on ways to incorporate technology in the classroom, with sample online resources for students and teachers. Chapter 8 encourages teachers to collaborate with other professionals in the school and in the community as a way to involve others in the learning process. Finally, Chapter 9 pulls everything together and offers suggestions for planning strategic and effective lessons for the English learners in your classroom.

It is quite clear that the future of our educational system in this country will be determined largely by our willingness and ability to help an increasingly diverse population of children who want and deserve the chance to achieve their dreams.

Acknowledgments

We would like to thank Rachel Livsey, Jessica Allan, and the editorial and production staff of Corwin Press who contributed to this book, as well as the following reviewers:

Randy Cook
Chemistry and Physics Teacher
Tri County High School
Howard City, MI

Gustava Cooper-Baker
Principal
Sanford B. Ladd African
    Centered School
Kansas City School District
Kansas City, MO

Holly A. Hitchcock
EL Teacher
School District of Clayton
Wydown Middle School
Clayton, MO

Gaetane Jean-Marie
Associate Professor
University of Oklahoma
Tulsa, OK

Noni Mendoza Reis
Professor and
    Department Chair
Department of Educational
    Leadership, College of
    Education
San José State University
San José, CA

About the Authors

Ellen Kottler, EdS, is currently a lecturer in the Department of Secondary Education at California State University, Fullerton. She received her EdS from the University of Nevada, Las Vegas in Instructional and Curricular Studies; her MA from Eastern Michigan University; and her BA from the University of Michigan. She has been a teacher in inner city schools as well as urban and rural settings. She also served as a curriculum specialist in social studies. Her areas of interest include beginning teacher support, social studies education, and supporting English language learners in the classroom. She is the author or coauthor of several articles and books for educators, including *Secrets to Success for Social Studies Teachers, Counseling Skills for Teachers, Secrets to Success for Beginning Elementary Teachers, On Being a Teacher,* and *Secrets for Secondary School Teachers: How to Succeed in Your First Year.*

Jeffrey A. Kottler, PhD, is Professor and Chair of the Counseling Department at California State University, Fullerton. He is the author of more than 65 books on education, counseling, and general nonfiction, including a dozen texts (*Introduction to Counseling, Stress Management and Prevention, Counseling Skills for Teachers*) and another dozen books on the nature of change (*On Being a Therapist, What You Never Learned in Graduate School, Growing a Therapist, Making Changes Last*) and teaching (*On Being a Teacher, Classrooms Under the Influence, Succeeding With Difficult*

Students). He has also authored several books that describe rather complex phenomena in highly accessible prose (*Travel That Can Change Your Life, Private Moments, Secret Selves,* and *The Language of Tears*). His books have been translated into more than a dozen languages.

Jeffrey is Founder of the Madhav Ghimire Foundation, which is devoted to helping prevent sex slavery in Nepal by supporting the education of girls at risk who could not otherwise attend school.

Chris Street, PhD, is Associate Professor of Secondary Education at California State University, Fullerton. He received his PhD from the University of Texas, Austin. He earned his MA from California State University, San Diego and his BA from the University of California, Santa Barbara. Chris has taught English language learners at both the middle school and college levels. He currently serves on the editorial advisory board for the *Journal of Content Area Reading* and is a teacher consultant with the National Writing Project. His research interests include adolescent literacy and the teaching of reading and writing. His work has appeared in a variety of journals and books, including *Teacher Education Quarterly, The Social Studies, Journal of Content Area Reading, Multicultural Education, Journal of College Reading and Learning, Journal of Adolescent & Adult Literacy,* and *Comprehending Nonfiction 6–8.*

CHAPTER ONE

Getting to Know the Student

M iguel, a new arrival in your classroom, has been with you for the past week. While the other children are working on an assignment, you notice that he is intensely occupied looking around the room. Wanting to offer him all the encouragement you can, you approach his desk and ask if he needs any help. At first he looks at you with a blank stare; then he hesitates a moment longer and shakes his head. His eyes move back to the page on his desk in front of him. As soon as you turn your back, his eyes resume their travels around the room.

You sit at your desk confused by this interaction. Did Miguel understand what you asked him? Does he have any idea what is going on with the assignment? How are you supposed to help him when you can't even communicate in such a way that he will respond? Does he have some learning disabilities or perhaps some deficit in his social skills? You notice he has yet to interact with the other children. How are you supposed to make any of these determinations when you are not even aware of the extent of his English communication and comprehension?

SENSITIVITY TO CULTURAL AND LINGUISTIC DIFFERENCES

One in five persons living in the United States speaks a language other than English at home. In particular areas of the country,

1

such as California and Texas, native English speakers are actually outnumbered by those who speak another language at home. This trend can be traced to a number of patterns—shifting populations throughout North America; increased immigration, especially from Latin America and Southeast Asia; and rising birthrates of non-English-proficient or limited-English-proficient populations. In fact, more immigrants arrived in the United States in the 1990s than during any other decade in history (Gray & Fleischman, 2005).

Immigration Patterns

Each year the United States is becoming increasingly ethnically and linguistically diverse, with more than 90 percent of recent immigrants coming from non-English-speaking countries (Echevarria, Vogt, & Short, 2004). The Latino population, for example, is predicted to reach 24 percent of the general population by 2050. Likewise, Asian Americans will represent approximately 10 percent of the population by 2050 (Lindholm-Leary, 2005). With these immigration trends, it is not surprising that English learners are the fastest-growing population group in U.S. public schools (Lachat, 2004).

These shifting demographics have really changed the educational landscape. The percentage of public school students who are racial/ethnic minorities increased from 22 percent in 1972 to 42 percent in 2003, primarily due to growth in Latino enrollments (National Center for Education Statistics, 2005). Moreover, in 2003 minority public school enrollment (54 percent) exceeded White enrollment (46 percent) in the West, while the number of children ages 5–17 who spoke a language other than English at home more than doubled between 1979 and 2003. Among these children, the number who spoke English with difficulty (i.e., did not speak English "very well") also grew strikingly during this period. For both of these groups of children, Spanish was the language most frequently spoken at home (National Center for Education Statistics, 2005).

Whereas for the most part, earlier immigrants came from Europe, newcomers now arrive primarily from Asia, Mexico, and Central and South America. If future trends in immigration follow past patterns, it can be expected that the majority of our school-age children will continue to come from Latin America and Asia.

Based on 2000 census data (U.S. Census Bureau, 2000), newcomers to America arrived most frequently from Latin America (51 percent), Asia (27 percent), and Europe (17 percent), with 5 percent of the total listed as "other."

Based on these same census data, we know that most of these immigrants settled in the following states: California (Los Angeles/Orange County, San Francisco Bay Area), New York (New York City), Florida (Miami), and Texas (Houston), although other places, such as Boston, Washington, D.C., and many Midwestern cities, have also seen an influx of immigrants.

Furthermore, the diversity of immigration patterns is not evenly distributed across the country. For years the majority of the country's immigrants has settled in California, Texas, and New York, but now newcomers from other countries have begun to settle throughout the United States, integrating into rural, urban, and suburban settings, even in small towns that have never before experienced many newcomers, much less those who come from a foreign country. In fact, Southern and Midwestern states are showing some of the greatest changes in K–12 enrollment of English learners (Lachat, 2004). Schools in Midwestern states, such as Iowa and Nebraska, now provide educational services for English learners. Iowa, for example, has seen its English learner population increase more than 200 percent, while Kansas experienced a 350 percent increase in the numbers of English learners receiving an education during the 1990s (Office of English Language Acquisition, Language Enhancement, and Academic Achievement for Limited English Proficient Students, 2002a, 2002b). According to the U.S. Department of Education, 19 states have reported increases of between 50 and 200 percent of English learners from 2000 to 2003 (U.S. Department of Education, 2003). With changes such as these occurring throughout the country, it is easy to assume that almost every community will see a significant increase of newcomers from abroad.

New Challenges and Responsibilities

Obviously, some of your students will be members of minority groups who are multilingual in languages other than English; others will have minimal language proficiency, which could hinder their ability to be academically or socially successful.

Whichever the case, you are going to face increased numbers of students with limited English-speaking ability, adding new challenges to your teaching responsibilities.

The challenges posed by working with increasing numbers of English learners are even more pressing in light of the No Child Left Behind Act (NCLB) of 2001, which mandates that *all* students meet high academic standards (Faltis & Coulter, 2007). By requiring that all schools hold all students accountable to high academic standards, NCLB has the potential to enhance educational equity. Yet you may be wondering just how to best meet the needs of your English learners. This book was written to help you to both support your English learners while also challenging them to reach the high academic standards required of all students in public schools.

We began this chapter by observing one student, Miguel, whose behavior appeared confusing. Upon some reflection, you have noticed that he smiles when he enters the room. He seems shy and rarely speaks, but you believe that is to be expected, given the new situation he finds himself in. You note that he follows the other children in carrying out routines, yet his schoolwork has been minimal.

When you consider the possible reasons to account for his lack of compliance, you realize that you actually know very little about him. How did he end up where he is? Where did he come from? What is important to him? What does he think about when he is daydreaming? How does he feel inside? You resolve to find some way to get to know him better. In order to carry out an effective plan for any of your students, you will need to assess the skills, abilities, and interests they bring to the classroom, with special attention to their cultural background and language proficiency.

When Teachers Become Students

In the collection of diverse peoples who make up North America, it has become more and more important to be sensitive to individual learning styles, communication patterns, and interaction styles that are reflective of various cultures. Thus the approach you might take with a Mexican American student would be quite different from one you would choose with a child from Bosnia or a new arrival from Korea or India. Before you can ever expect to reach any of the children with limited English speaking proficiency in your class, you must first become a functional expert in their backgrounds. Such an expertise will provide a foundation from which to structure your teaching efforts.

As one example, a teacher felt frustrated with the lack of progress he had been making with an Inuit child from East Greenland. Not only had the girl failed to develop much proficiency in the English language, but she seemed to manifest serious attention deficit problems and would frequently get out of her seat of her own accord and wander about the room.

Before making a referral to special education or the school psychologist for an assessment, the teacher decided to do a little research on his own. After studying a bit about East Greenlandic culture, he realized that the children from her region were rarely given much structure or discipline, because it was believed they carried the spirits of old people and so should be treated with great respect. It was very common for school to be quite "fluid," with children frequently up and about whenever the mood suited them. Furthermore, because Danish was the official language of Greenland, and West Greenlandic was the language of instruction in the schools, an East Greenlandic child was already expected to learn three languages in order to function effectively. In some cases, there was considerable resistance to having to learn another one, especially in such a strange world where students were forced to remain still for long periods of time.

Once the teacher had taken the time to learn some background about the cultural origins of this student (and others), he was able to demonstrate much greater understanding and sensitivity to behavior that previously had appeared to him as disruptive, uncooperative, or unmotivated. A student's language acquisition and proficiency are thus directly related to the teacher's cultural proficiency, that is, the ability to adapt the classroom and school environments in such a way that individual needs are recognized and responded to effectively (Robins, Lindsey, Lindsey, & Terrell, 2002).

IDENTIFYING TERMS

Before going any farther, it is necessary to address how the student will be described. There has been, and continues to be, much discussion in the field related to selection of a term to identify this population of people who are not native English speakers but who are learning the English language (Cary, 2000; Reiss, 2001, 2008). In the first edition of this book, the prevailing term used by teachers to describe children was *English as a second language (ESL) students.* However, for many children, English is not their second language; it is their third, fourth, or one of many languages they are learning. Therefore, ESL is not a fitting label.

As of this writing, the term most commonly used is *English language learners (ELL).* This, too, has its problems, as all children in the United States are learning English. The term *bilingual students* is sometimes used as well, but the problem is that this term implies the students can read, write, and speak in both languages equally. *Language minority students* is another term that does not work well, because in some areas the number of students learning English will be in the majority. For the purpose of this book, the term *English learners* will be used as a way to describe those students whose English is limited in comparison to what would be considered developmentally appropriate for a native English-speaking child with English-speaking parents. This description is meant to be a temporary, not permanent, descriptor and is used to indicate the current language ability of students, with no reflection on their potential.

RELATIONSHIPS ARE EVERYTHING

So much about learning is influenced by the quality of the relationships you develop with students. When children trust and respect you, when they know you care about them, when they like you and what you stand for, they will learn almost anything you want to teach (Mawhinney & Sagan, 2007; Kottler, Zehm, & Kottler, 2005; Moje, 1996; Street, 2005a, 2005b). On the other hand, if students believe teachers are unfair or mean or unduly critical, it is very difficult to make much progress.

Trusting Relationships

Nonnative English speakers may have very good reasons to mistrust the motives of teachers and other authority figures, especially if these professionals are members of the dominant culture. They may have suffered injustices in the past or been subjected to discrimination. They may have heard stories (some true, some exaggerations and distortions) that lead them to be cautious and hesitant.

Yet once teachers develop caring relationships with students, many benefits often follow:

1. Students are willing to take risks without fear of being humiliated.

2. When students are confused or do not understand something, they are more willing to ask for help.

3. Students may be more willing to show caring and respect for one another if the teacher models these same values during daily interactions.

4. Students may disclose more about their lives and be more honest about their innermost thoughts and feelings when they believe they will be accepted and valued.

5. Both students and their teachers experience greater trust, intimacy, and respect in their relationships, making the school experience more satisfying and fulfilling.

The Value of Relationship Skills

Relationship skills are not often taught in teacher preparation programs, which tend to heavily emphasize content areas, curricular issues, technological innovations, and pedagogical methods. Yet there are probably few strategies more powerful and effective in building successful collaborations than those behaviors designed to deepen relationships (Kottler & Kottler, 2007). These include, but are not limited to, the following.

Communicating Constructive Attitudes

Most students (or anyone else for that matter) have a secret fear that they will be judged critically. It is very important to present yourself to students as open, accessible, and nonjudgmental. This means that although you may not approve of certain behaviors that are disruptive or counterproductive, you do not write off the students, as people, just because you do not like their annoying behavior.

Demonstrating Effective "Attending" Behaviors

This means presenting yourself to students as a good listener. You show this through your body posture, eye contact, and facial expressions, communicating your intense interest in what they have to say. It is actually quite rare that people give others their truly undivided attention. Because learning and speaking a language involve far more than merely articulating verbal expression, teachers have the opportunity to model appropriate listening skills in their own behavior.

Asking Open-Ended Questions

This is the type of query that is designed to foster exploration rather than to cut off communication. Compare, for instance, two questions worded in very different ways:

Closed-Ended Question

Teacher: So Miguel, did you have a good time with your family this weekend?

Student: Sí.

Open-Ended Question

Teacher: Miguel, what did you do with your family this weekend?

Notice that closed questions can be answered in single-word responses, whereas open questions encourage elaboration. If there is one mistake that teachers make most often when trying to be helpful, it is in the area of questioning, where they may come across as interrogating rather than showing interest.

Listening Actively

Students who are already self-conscious about their ability to communicate in a new language need lots of reassurance that they have been heard and understood. Demonstrate ways to listen actively through nonverbal and verbal acknowledgments. This includes such things as

1. Smiling and using facial expressions to communicate interest and responsiveness
2. Nodding your head frequently to indicate that you are tracking
3. Using your body posture to face the person fully and show your interest

Reflecting Back What You Heard

One way to prove that you have not only heard what was said but also understood its deeper meaning is by reflecting back both the content and the underlying feeling of the message. Note the way the teacher does this with a student frustrated about a grade on an assignment:

Student: This grade isn't fair.

Teacher: You're frustrated because you worked hard on this assignment and you still got what you think is a poor grade.

Student: [Nods her head]

Teacher: [Waits patiently]

Student: I spent a lot of time on this. And you still think it stinks.

Teacher: No matter how hard you try, it still seems like it won't make a bit of difference.

In this brief dialogue, the specifics are less important than the very idea that the teacher is trying hard to validate the student's feelings rather than defending herself and her grading policy. She keeps the focus on the student and his feelings, reinforcing his willingness to express himself in English.

Each of these relationship skills is designed to encourage greater communication as well as to help students feel heard and understood. Any of the methods described in the following chapters will work much better if it occurs within the context of constructive, caring relationships.

UNDERSTAND THE STUDENT'S WORLD

The first phase in any helping effort involves learning about the person you intend to reach. All communication is based on sensitivity to a person's needs, as well as an understanding of the individual's unique world. It is sometimes difficult to fully comprehend what it must be like to live in a place ruled by constant fear of making mistakes.

One student relates his first experience coming to America. He was on a flight from Mexico City to Seattle, his first time ever on an airplane. He was on his way to live with family members who worked as migrant workers in the fruit orchards of central Washington's Yakima Valley. He didn't speak a word of English.

The boy found himself in a window seat. Rather than feeling privileged and awed by the view of his soon-to-be adopted country out the window, he was feeling increasingly uncomfortable. He had to go to the bathroom very badly, but he was trapped in his seat by the passenger in the aisle seat on his right. He looked over and saw a well-dressed American businessman working diligently on his laptop computer. The boy decided he was some sort of important executive because he wore a suit jacket and a tie that was not even loosened at his neck. He must be working on something very important.

Fearful of interrupting this important man, the boy suffered silently in his seat with his legs crossed. Even if he had wanted to leave his seat to go to the toilet, he had no idea how to ask such a thing in English. He rehearsed, "*Permiso*" and "*Perdoname,*" but it didn't seem right to speak Spanish to such an important man. Instead, this boy recalls that his very first experience on his trip to America was to pee in his pants because he had been too afraid to ask permission to leave his seat. He couldn't communicate even his most basic needs.

It is sometimes hard for us to imagine that anyone could feel so afraid, so ashamed, so reluctant to speak at all, that a student would remain mute. But that is often the experience that nonnative language speakers report, and until you are able to understand what this is like, you have no chance of ever reaching them.

Before you can ever hope to connect with and influence a child, you must also know about what he or she considers most important. This background information involves not only assessing academic skills in verbal or quantitative areas, but also learning about family, cultural, and social customs that are an integral part of the child's life.

Here are a number of suggestions for getting to know your students. What makes many of these strategies so helpful is that they do not require a high level of language proficiency to get started.

Communicate With Pictures

One favorite technique of therapists is to ask new clients during a first interview to show photographs of family members as they are talking about their living situations. This accomplishes several tasks at the same time: (1) It creates an immediate sense of intimacy, because photos reveal one's most important influences; (2) it helps the professional to associate names with faces; and (3) it provides clues about family relationships that may prove useful when the time comes to understand better what is going on at home.

With English learners, photographs provide another advantage in that they don't require much verbal elaboration to have personal meaning. Photographs can be used as an alternative means of communication (although the same images may be interpreted differently based on cultural perceptions). Students may thus be invited to bring in photos of events that hold particular importance to them or that show individuals who are most significant to them.

In addition, photos can be taken periodically throughout the school year, capturing moments in time. They can be easily displayed. They serve as reminders to the student of how he or she felt at the beginning of school and how initial impressions and feelings have changed. You can take pictures of the student to record participation in different activities—playing a part in a skit, painting a wall mural, solving a math problem on the board, working on a cooperative learning task, interacting with other children in the lunchroom. Pictures can be taken of projects that are too big to keep in the classroom on a permanent basis.

Pictures are also an excellent way of communicating to parents and families what happens during the school day. Giving children pictures of the students and teachers in the classroom will provide them with ways to take the events of the school day home to share with parents, brothers and sisters, extended family, and friends.

One teacher who specializes in working with students from diverse backgrounds explains:

> I think parents feel more comfortable when they see what takes place in school. They are curious about what their children do and with whom they spend time. I make sure to indicate the dates the pictures are taken so they can see the progress children make over time.

Students can also be invited to bring in pictures of themselves and their families to share with the class. These can be used for get-acquainted activities, to stimulate speech or writing assignments, and to build self-esteem. Most of all, they allow children to help educate others about the unique circumstances in which they live. Among Maori and other indigenous children, for example, their individual names are relatively less important to their families than the mountain and river near where they are from. This, in fact, makes an interesting class activity, in which students are invited to introduce themselves in the Maori way by first talking about the "boat" that brought them to this land (this is a metaphor for their family journey to this time and place), then describing the features of nature that they identify with most strongly, and then finally introducing their family and how it is unique.

The teacher demonstrates this method as follows:

> My parents immigrated to this country after World War II. They were Jewish refugees who survived the Holocaust—that is when the Nazis put people of my religion, as well as others, into special camps where they worked as slaves. The boat they arrived on was filled with similar people who were all poor and sick.
>
> After arriving in New York, they made their way to Detroit—that is a city in the Midwest that is known for making cars. My river where I come from is called the Detroit River, and there is no mountain nearby, but if I had to choose one, I'd pick Pine Knob, which is a ski hill where I used to play as a child.
>
> My family worked in the automotive factories in a number of different jobs. My last name is of Russian origin, and my middle name is Swedish, because my mother's family came from Sweden.

Obviously, English learners will have trouble being so detailed in their introductions, so options can be created whereby they tell their stories using props, maps, photos, music, and native foods, or even bringing in a family member as a guest.

Although videotaping has some special advantages over still photographs, it presents a few additional problems. Students with limited language proficiency may find it difficult to speak under such "performance" conditions. Until the student is comfortable with the taping process, time in front of the camera should be limited.

Develop a Portfolio

Developing a record of the child's progress in school is an important first step toward getting to know the student. Several resources (MacDonald, 1998; Schurr, 1999) are helpful in guiding your efforts to study systematically a student's performance across a wide range of activities. Make a list of everything the child can do without using language—build, sort, match, categorize, sequence, copy, draw, listen to music, look at pictures, mimic, pantomime. Then, look for examples of listening, speaking, reading, and writing. If time and opportunity permit, try to observe student behavior in more "natural" settings, because some of the most effective interactions you can ever have with a child are in the hallways, on the playground, or in more informal places.

With respect to using English, as unobtrusively as possible, notice and categorize mistakes. Are there pronunciation errors, grammatical and syntactical errors, or comprehension and semantic errors? These are to be expected with beginning students. Include notes from your observations of interactions with other people, samples of student work, descriptions of projects and pictures, as well as grades and standardized test results you receive.

Analyze which instructional activities the student enjoys most. Which activities does the student try to avoid? Could these preferences be a reflection of cultural values? For example, does the student prefer cooperative learning exercises rather than those that require competition? Or does the child prefer to work alone?

Not only will a portfolio provide a structure for tracking student experiences and progress, but it will also give you a well-rounded picture of the student. Portfolio items will give you a wide variety of material to present at parent conferences, and you will also be able to provide the student with a record of the progress made in your class.

Inquire Into Student Interests

Take your explorations one step further and find out what activities the child pursues outside school. Does the student like to hike, cook, or fix bicycles? Is the student a member of a scouting organization, a religious group, or an athletic team? Does the student have a pet or like to draw? Does the student belong to a choir, band, or other school club? Mawhinney and Sagan (2007) suggest using interest surveys or other introductory activities to learn students' interests.

A turning point occurred with a high school student when one teacher discovered that the student played sports.

I found out Raul was a soccer player and went to watch the team practice one day after school. The next day in class, I started a conversation with him about the team. At first he didn't answer, but then he smiled. I could tell he felt good that I had taken the time to learn about something important to him. Everything sort of fell into place after that. He became more responsive to me personally and more interested and active in class.

What does the student do when he or she is alone? By identifying the child's interests and skills, you can later relate lessons to topics the child will be able to identify with and build on the knowledge base already established.

An eighth-grade teacher shares this example:

I had a young girl who came directly from Mexico the summer before school began. Since she spoke some English, she was put in my developmental English class. She was a good student who was eager to learn, but her grasp of writing English was quite limited. Fragments. No subject-verb agreement. Incorrectly placed modifiers. You get the picture. We spent a lot of time reading, writing, and working on grammar.

In December, the school received tickets to attend the Ballet Folklorico. It was a wonderful evening that all who attended enjoyed. The next day, the assignment was to write about the experience from the previous evening. When she called me over to read her rough draft, I was moved to tears. It was the most beautifully written memory I had read, and it was perfectly punctuated! An English teacher's dream. I learned that to truly get the best from our students, teachers must make the assignments meaningful so that students want to show off what the teacher has helped them learn.

EXPLORE THE STUDENT'S FAMILY BACKGROUND

To learn about the student's family background, plan information-seeking activities. For example, through geography lessons students may share where they came from, whether it was a rural or urban setting, and the length of time they have spent in this country.

Listen to the Stories Students Tell

During one-on-one conversations you may learn a lot more about why the family immigrated to North America in the first place. Was it for better economic opportunities? Were they escaping some sort of persecution or physical threats? Of course, you would wish to be very sensitive in the way you respond to this subject, because there may be shame, guilt, or legal problems associated with the immigration.

When one professor was teaching a university honors seminar, he discovered that more than half the class had been in this country fewer than 10 years. But what was really surprising was the number of students who had suffered terribly in their countries of origin. Several students escaped abject poverty. One Cambodian student had watched her family murdered before her eyes. Several others narrowly escaped life-threatening incidents, and all these early experiences significantly affected their learning in school and mastery of their new language. Because all these students were high achievers, they had actually demonstrated tremendous resilience as a result of early traumas. They reported that their teachers made a huge difference in helping them put the past behind them and channel their energies toward productive directions. Many of their siblings had not been nearly so fortunate.

Through the use of pictures, as mentioned earlier, you can find out how many brothers and sisters are in the family, their ages and sexes, whether they attend school or not, and whether extended family members live in the household. Through conversation, you can learn the lines of authority in the family and the patterns of socialization.

At the elementary school level, this information can be elicited through discussion of the family, counting and sorting activities, or responses to children's literature. At the secondary level, the information can be collected through discussion of immigration in a social studies class, the family in a home economics class, genetics in a science class, the concept of role in a sociology class, or reaction to a reading in an English class. Lessons on multicultural topics, such as relationships, legends, customs, power, and authority, can be incorporated into the curriculum.

Once students develop some degree of fluency as writers, they can express their ideas through writing assignments, such as journals and autobiographies. Those who are not yet proficient in their writing can instead draw pictures to respond to questions or express themselves. One of the best assignments for any age group—also favored by counselors and therapists who are attempting to learn about children's experiences—is to ask them to draw pictures of themselves with their families. Through words, gestures, dramatic enactments, or further drawings, they can then be encouraged to talk about their families.

Learning about the student's position in the family and assigned household responsibilities will give you insight into behavior at school and after school. Does the child care for younger brothers and sisters or elderly grandparents? Does the child cook and clean for the family? Does the child work to support the family? These responsibilities will limit the student's involvement in school as well as in community activities. For example, the student may not have time or money to come to a spaghetti dinner fundraiser, talent show, or extracurricular activities. However, you will become aware of the students who are capable of fulfilling leadership roles, those who are nurturing, and those who are capable of taking on tasks requiring responsibility in the classroom.

In the example that began this chapter, Miguel disclosed, through gestures and halting English, that he was left alone much of the time. His parents both worked long hours, leaving him to take care of the house. He was able to communicate that he did understand much of what was said to him. He had been watching a lot of television, especially music videos, and he found that by memorizing the words to the songs, his ear was becoming more accustomed to English. He very much wanted to do his homework, but he was just too busy with things that he had to do around the house. In his spare time—what little he could find—he had started playing around with a harmonica. Music seemed to be an important part of his life.

Exploring the area of home responsibilities will also give you an arena in which to converse with students and give them opportunities to practice speaking English in a private setting with you. Just think about how self-conscious you might feel using your limited proficiency in another language when speaking with native speakers in their country. Children may thus be more willing to try out their own limited English if they trust you and feel that you are not judging them.

Furthermore, the children have the opportunity to show off what they are most proud of—baby sister, new puppy, knowledge of their native history, cooking skills, or harmonica playing. This can later be shared with the class in small groups or even in the whole community as confidence grows.

Visit the Home

Too often, teachers may fail to include or discount the wisdom and ways of learning that students bring with them to school. In particular, the knowledge and cultural resources of diverse students may be disregarded or go unnoticed rather than being seen as assets. By engaging in home visits, teachers can gain familiarity with these resources and use them strategically in the classroom.

Following research on literacy practices in Latino homes, Luis Moll and his colleagues (1992) encouraged teachers to do their own research in the homes of their students to learn how family members share knowledge with each other. In this Funds of Knowledge for Teaching Project, Moll led university professors and teams of teachers to discuss their findings and how they might incorporate the families' funds of knowledge into the school curriculum.

These visits also served as a way to build trust among the teachers, parents, and students while developing a sense of community. Moving beyond the walls of the classroom enabled teachers to get to know families on a personal level and acquire knowledge that they would not otherwise have been able to access. Ginsberg (2007) suggests teachers not only identify and practice asking questions respectfully ahead of time, but also practice taking two-column field notes (responses to questions on one side and inter-viewer's reaction on the other). Later, teachers can add to any notes taken during the visit, note any personal assumptions, and share thoughts with others. They can then work together to develop a "funds of knowledge" chart on the knowledge and skills of the family and/or cultural group in general categories based on what teachers see in the home. Teachers then note the strengths of their students while developing respect for each individual.

Whether in a formal program, such as those described above, or informally with colleagues, the value of making home visits is immeasurable. You may need the help of translators or transla-tion software, so check with your school for administrative guid-ance and support. And don't overlook opportunities to write grants to secure funding for projects such as this one. With advance plan-ning, several teachers can visit many different families together in an afternoon.

Using Writing as a Window

Teachers need to get to know their students on a personal basis. But especially for secondary teachers—who may have responsibility for more than 150 students—this is difficult to do. As a practical reality, it is not likely that secondary teachers will have the opportunity to conduct home visits for more than a handful of their students. However, by asking students to write about their household "funds of knowledge," teachers can "validate the back-ground knowledge with which students come equipped" (Gonzalez, 1995, p. 5).

Research on writing attitudes reveals that many students are uninterested in writing about topics that have no personal con-nection to them (Mayher, 1990; Street, 2002, 2003). Using writ-ing as a window into students' areas of intelligence and hidden talents is a tactical way to learn more about what our students know and who they consult for help with academic tasks. Norma Gonzalez (1995) suggests that teaching is more effective when teachers learn more about their individual students and their lives outside of school. As they write, students inform their teachers of their history, particular life situations, and interests while at the same time improving their writing skills. This work is beginning to occur with students at both the elementary and secondary levels (Amanti, 1995; Fisher & Frey, 2003; Gonzalez, 1995; Stock, 1995). Tapping the funds of knowledge of English learners—which are often hidden at the secondary level—is especially important, since many of these students avoid writing due to their feelings of inadequacy as writers.

Simply offering students the opportunity to choose their own writing topics allowed one writing teacher to make his students' experiences the foundation of his middle school composition class. He called this approach the Funds of Knowledge Writing Project.

> I asked my students to write about topics of interest to them and they immediately felt a sense of acceptance in the classroom. I provided them with supportive feedback on their writing as mutual trust slowly developed. I also noticed that the dynamics in my classroom changed. I moved about the room talking to students about their work and assisting as needed. Students liked choosing their own topics and shared what they cared about and what their dreams were.
>
> When the students became my teachers, I learned many important lessons about the cultural and familial resources of my students. Juanita would be the first person in her family to attend college. Jesus described his family's role in the Guatemalan government before coming to the United States. Norma began a successful letter writing campaign to repair the elevators in her building. (Street, 2005a)

In this way, writing served as a culturally relevant teaching strategy that not only improved the literacy skills of his students but also enabled the teacher to get to know them on a personal level and engage them in powerful learning.

Invite Parents to Participate in Your Class

There are many ways to include parents in the classroom. Many teachers ask for volunteers at the beginning of the school year to help with special events or make presentations to students.

Other teachers send out surveys with a list of topics and issues to be covered in their class. Parents and grandparents can serve as an audience for a presentation or demonstration, chaperone a field trip, help with a special class activity, or share their special skills, life experiences, or private collections to augment your curriculum. Boothe (2000) emphasizes having family members serve as cultural experts—with clothing, music, and food, for example—or showcase their own areas of expertise through classroom demonstrations. Check on the procedures at your schools for inviting guest speakers and involving volunteers in the classroom.

Many teachers have written about the benefits of inviting family members to share their own areas of expertise with students. For example, Marla Hensley, a kindergarten teacher, shares how she learned that a father of one of her students, Mr. Jarman, was a musician. After visiting his home and noticing a guitar leaning against the closet, she asked him if he would like to share his music in the classroom. One visit became two, and two became three, and by the end of the school year, Mr. Jarman had written and directed a musical for the kindergarten. Not only did Marla's students benefit from Mr. Jarman's knowledge, but she transcended the typical teacher-parent relationship. As she explains, "A friend-to-friend interchange and sense of common purpose are fostered" (Hensley, 1995, p. 16) in home-school relationships such as these.

Other teachers have shared stories of their successful experiences with reaching out to students' families. One writes of how he involved his fifth graders as ethnographers in the classroom by asking them to develop a survey of the languages spoken in the school as part of a social studies lesson (Craig, 1994) while a special education teacher chronicles a major breakthrough that was achieved with a hard-to-reach student by using the student's home experiences in the classroom (Gittings, 1995).

Determine the Home
Attitude Toward Learning English

A home language survey is completed when students are enrolled in school. If parents indicate that they speak a language other than English, the student will be tested for proficiency in English and for his or her primary language proficiency. With your English learners, you may be able to find out if people in the home speak English in order to have some idea if there is additional support available. If nobody else in the home speaks English well, that may guide your efforts to develop alternative support systems to provide students assistance with schoolwork and language support.

It is also important to find out what the attitude is among family members toward learning English. In two different Arab American families, for example, quite different messages were given at home. In one case, the child's entire family was attempting to learn English together; the whole process of learning English became a fun, challenging activity that brought them closer together. The family watched situation comedies on television at night and tried to talk about what happened in English. The child in this situation received a strong message from his parents: If you want to succeed in this country you must speak English perfectly.

In another case, the family atmosphere emphasized much more the importance of maintaining their cultural roots. Arabic was the only language encouraged at home. Because the parents both lived and worked in an exclusively Arab community, English remained a "foreign" language. In fact, it was entirely possible for members of this community to live their whole lives speaking only their native language. The message thus communicated to the child was: Speak English only if you must, but Arabic is your real tongue.

It is not uncommon for first-generation immigrants to feel that learning English is not important and to resent the new language and customs of the United States. Second-generation immigrants may also feel that their parents have been successful without learning English and that there is no reason for them to be any different. If they are from a community where others speak their language, they may prefer to speak in the language with which they feel most comfortable, the first language. Even at school, speaking English can easily be avoided.

Many new immigrants have left behind all that is familiar; all they have remaining is their own language. As in the case of the first Arab American example, others may see speaking English as a vital survival skill and refuse to speak native languages in the home. This, of course, presents its own problems, because then the children may lose much of their ethnic heritage. They may experience internal conflicts, loss of cultural identity, and marginalization among those of their own background (Robinson & Howard-Hamilton, 2000).

There are certain tribes of Native Americans, for example, in which no one speaks the native language any longer. The children have lost the opportunity to connect with their past even if they wanted to. Among a band of Paiutes in one local area, one child expressed an interest in learning his native dialect. Unfortunately, there was nobody within the group who remembered enough of the language to teach it.

Determine the Stage of Acculturation

Children will develop different attitudes toward learning English based on how long they have been in the country and where they fall in the *continuum of acculturation,* a concept that describes the process by which members of minority groups become socialized into accepting the values of the dominant culture (Berry & Sam, 1997). Although the progression through the process of acculturation varies from individual to individual, several stages have been identified (Atkinson, Morten, & Sue, 1997). At first, children may be quite excited. Everything is novel. Each day is a new experience. Then the students experience culture shock. Students feel frustrated by their efforts as they begin to adapt to the ways of the new culture. In the next stage, students ideally gain more control and are more successful. They begin to adjust to school, and English language skills improve rapidly. In the final stage, students adjust fully to the new culture, ideally retaining their close association to their family and cultural roots.

The ease with which children move through the stages depends on the degree of contrast between cultures and the amount of discrimination faced by their cultural group. Family factors include the reasons for immigration, the degree of separation from the family, and the disruption of economic status. Personal factors include the age of the child, gender, language fluency, attitudes and personality characteristics, and the nature of prior formal education. Younger children have an easier time than adolescents, as they have had less opportunity for their native cultural values, beliefs, and customs to become embedded. Females from developing nations are likely to pursue domestic responsibilities rather than higher education. Students who develop communication skills, exhibit flexibility, and can build relationships will be able to adapt more quickly than those who do not. Positive attitudes toward education and the new culture, as well as an openness to new ideas, are associated with acculturation and the development of bicultural competence (Vargas-Reighley, 2005). Personality characteristics such as patience, tolerance, self-confidence, and healthy self-esteem open the door, whereas perfectionism, rigidity, and self-centeredness make it difficult to adjust. Teachers are encouraged to see children as individuals and to be sensitive to the cultural values related to education, gender, and assimilation that students bring to the classroom.

PAY ATTENTION TO SOCIAL AND CULTURAL CUSTOMS

It is important to become aware of individual and cultural differences and how they may contribute to potential problems in the classroom through miscommunication. Doing an ethnographic study of your students will provide you with a wealth of information explaining their behavior and will give you insight into how best to help them in the classroom. Individuals differ on the following dimensions:

- Verbal communication (pronunciation, patterns of speech, tempo of speech, stress, and pitch)
- Nonverbal communication (eye contact, meaning of gestures)
- Proxemics (spatial distance between people; e.g., some people like to stand very close to one another, and backing away from them would be taken as an affront)
- Interpersonal touching (e.g., whether the student prefers a light or firm pat on the back)
- Attention span (ability and motivation to sustain interest)
- Orientation toward learning (e.g., preference for a quiet or noisy background)
- Social values (peer group influences)
- Intellectual orientation (e.g., is frequent questioning valued or discouraged?)

In considering the social and cultural background of your students, ask yourself the following questions:

1. Has the student been socialized to be an active participant or a passive recipient of information in the classroom?

2. How is the concept of time viewed? Is punctuality a virtue, or is time considered to be flexible?

3. Are students expected to make eye contact with their teachers, or to look down out of respect?

4. Do students nod their heads to be polite or to show they understand?

5. Do parents regard teachers as experts and refrain from expressing differences of opinion?

6. Is cooperation or competition encouraged?

7. Is the family patriarchal, restricting educational aspirations for female children?

8. Is education or work valued more in the family?

9. Do students expect specific directions for carrying out tasks and therefore have difficulty choosing their own learning activities?

10. Do students not ask questions because they have been taught not to bother adults?

11. Is the student expected to tell the teacher what the teacher wants to hear (e.g., that an assignment was completed when it hasn't even been started)?

12. Are expressions of emotions and feelings emphasized or hidden?

13. Are speaking or listening modes of communication preferred?

14. Do students exhibit low self-esteem and self-defeating behaviors because they feel they cannot succeed as a result of socioeconomic marginality and discrimination?

15. Is change considered inevitable and desirable, or is tradition revered?

In order to understand parent reactions and avoid misunderstanding or miscommunication, it is critical for the teacher to learn about the specific backgrounds of all their students and to inform parents of the expectations of American education. As Allington and Cunningham (1996) point out as one example, some parents may not understand the difference between books that are assigned as texts throughout the year and given to the student versus library books, which are "borrowed" and must be returned in a few weeks.

Scarcella (1990) encourages teachers to compare the values promoted by the mainstream middle class to those of other cultures. Values in the United States include such things as organized time, competitiveness and upward mobility, equality of opportunity, individualism, autonomy, and informality. Of course, even within the diverse regions of the United States, we can see huge differences between values on the East Coast versus the West Coast; between the North and the South; between rural areas versus urban areas; and among individual states, such as Texas, California, Vermont, Iowa, Mississippi, and Alaska.

One of the most common mistakes that beginners often make is forgetting that the differences within cultural groups can be greater than those between them. One can easily get in trouble by making generalizations or not knowing anything about people based on their cultural identity.

Each major cultural group, be it Asian or Latino, has differences in its subgroups, and cultures are always evolving. There are also differences among children due to the education and socioeconomic background of their parents, as well as the length of time spent and the nature of experience in the United States. As people become acculturated to their specific environment in the United States, they take on new values. For this reason, it is important to investigate the background of each student.

Effective teachers recognize that each student is unique. By focusing on individuals, teachers then personalize their instruction to meet the needs of their unique students. Effective teachers who focus on the learning strengths of their students and mediate the frequent mismatch between home and school cultures are engaging in "culturally responsive teaching" (Sadker, Sadker, & Zittleman, 2008), a practice that helps English learners to feel comfortable as they transition into their new classrooms.

Students will learn that certain behaviors are appropriate for school and others are expected at home, just as they learn that certain speech is acceptable on the street but not in the classroom. However, they may get confused about what to do or say in a given situation. Often students will develop two codes of conduct. One story in particular makes this point clear. A young boy was being disciplined by his mother. She had been very unhappy with something that he did. After she finished scolding him, he looked at her and said, "Am I supposed to look at you [as teachers at school request] or look away from you [as a sign of respect]? I can't remember."

Teachers must realize, too, that students will respond in very different ways to the pull between their two cultures. Some are eager and proud to adopt the new ways, whereas others are resentful and resistant. Yet others will vary from day to day.

You will find it valuable to learn about the cultural characteristics particular to your students (see Table 1.1). In some ways, this is the best part of your job—that you have the opportunity to learn not only from books but from the fascinating people you work with. Teachers must be aware of cultural differences in order to create a supportive environment. Facial expressions and gestures can be widely interpreted—even a smile can have different interpretations, from loving to cynical.

Just as you do not wish to misinterpret what your students' behavior means, neither do you want them to misread your gestures and actions. Discussing communication patterns—both verbal and nonverbal—with all your students will help everyone develop sensitivity to differences and similarities.

Table 1.1   Getting to Know Your Students

Strategies	Listen to individual stories
	Survey or interview students
	Look at students' photos
	Visit students' homes
	Use writing as a resource
	Invite parents to participate in the classroom
Topics to Explore	Previous schooling
	Student's interests and special skills
	Home attitude toward learning
	Past life experiences
	Stage of acculturation
	Social and cultural customs

To help English learners, we develop a sense of being socioculturally conscious (Villegas and Lucas, 2007). We begin by learning about the lives of our students, their cultures, and how they have been influenced by their experiences. As we respect and celebrate diversity, we then select strategies that will enable them to meet the high academic expectations we hold for all students.

SUGGESTED ACTIVITIES

1. Identify the English learners in your classroom. Develop a list of interview questions you would like to ask their parents related to student behavior.

2. Identify the values that you promote in your classroom. Compare this list to the values held by the students in your classroom from different backgrounds.

3. Observe an English learner in your classroom. Note how that child interacts with others in school—students, cafeteria staff, the principal, other teachers. Use this information to plan activities that will build on the student's strengths.

4. Reflect on times in your own educational experience when you felt mute, alienated, or isolated. Talk about these experiences in a small group of friends or classmates. Discuss what the common factors were that most contributed to your discomfort. Find a consensus about what helped you the most to come out of your shell and interact with others.

5. Generate a list of the ways in which you might invite parents of your students to get involved in your classroom. Use this list to plan activities that will build on the expertise of your students' parents.

CHAPTER TWO

Establishing a Comfortable Environment

Along with developing a positive relationship with students, effective teachers create and maintain the sort of classroom environment that will be safe, productive, and supportive. In the case of Miguel, introduced in the previous chapter, you might ask yourself several questions while considering this task: What can I do to help Miguel feel more comfortable in the classroom? How can I structure the learning environment to facilitate his development of English, as well as his mastery of the material in my curriculum? Just as important, how can I help him to like being at school, at least during the time that he is with me?

WELCOME STUDENTS TO YOUR ROOM

Encourage new students to come into the classroom with gentle, but not overbearing, enthusiasm. It cannot be overemphasized how important it is to learn to pronounce the students' names correctly. One student reports what a tremendous difference such an effort made to him:

> My name, Efraim, is difficult for many Anglos to get right. I don't make a big deal about it one way or another, but when I first came to this country, my teacher made me say my name over and

over until she could say it perfectly. She used to tease me that this was going to be her final examination and that I had her permission to correct her if she ever made a mistake. I can't tell you how much I appreciated that effort on her part. I really trusted her.

It also helps if you can learn a few phrases in the student's native language, so that you can greet him or her each day with a special welcome: *Ka hue?* ("What's happening?" in Fijian); *Apa khabar?* ("How are you?" in Malaysian); *Gracias por hacer un esferuzo.* ("Thank you for making an effort," in Spanish); *Seu trabalho e excelente.* ("Your work is excellent," in Portuguese). Reaching out to students in this way may be the most important thing you do, as it communicates your interest and caring toward students who may otherwise feel marginalized.

Look for clues in the student's behavior about what will make him or her feel most comfortable. Does the student cling to your side or stand independently away? Does the student speak freely, or just give a nod of the head? Do you need to assign a partner to stay with the child for a few days and guide him or her through the myriad of school day activities?

Picture yourself in the child's position—what would help *you* to feel more at ease in the school? Imagine that you are living in a strange, new place where almost everything familiar to you is now gone. You don't understand the rules, can't comprehend what people around you are saying, and can't even ask for the things you need most. You feel scared, lonely, and lost. You don't have many friends and have no idea how to go about making that happen. You live in terror that you will do or say the wrong thing and not only humiliate yourself beyond repair, but bring shame to your family and ancestors. You feel stupid and inadequate. Even worse: you feel no hope. You can't imagine that things will ever get better; you are doomed to spend your life in this place in which you can't even make sense of what is going on around you.

Now, get outside your own skin and crawl into the world of this child. Based on what you already know and understand about his or her experience, background, and personality, what might make the most difference?

Modeling Risk Taking

It is interesting that teachers are so eager for students to take constructive risks with their learning, but we often show reluctance to do the same ourselves. We also play it safe and embrace caution because we do not want to make a mistake or appear clueless. One of the misconceptions that some teachers hold is that if you can't get it right the first time, you should wait until you can select the perfect intervention. This is not only inhibiting but inadvisable.

In school, we often learned that when faced with questions, there were only four multiple-choice answers, one of which was correct and the others wrong. Success was simply a matter of selecting the correct option from among those presented. Then we get out into the real world, where not only are the choices limitless, but there is often no way to figure out which is the correct one. In any given situation, there are a dozen different things you could do or say, any of which might work fairly well. Even after the episode is over, it is still nearly impossible to figure out if your intervention was the best alternative.

The good news, however, is that it often does not matter so much if what you did was perfectly effective or the absolute best intervention. If you can develop a trusting, respectful relationship with your students, they will give you the benefit of the doubt when you mess up or make mistakes. Also, if you are willing to model taking risks, as well as owning your misjudgments, you make it much easier for students to do the same.

Your job is to provide students with a comfortable space to sit and work and the supplies necessary to complete their assignments. You can do this by eliminating distractions as much as possible. Introduce the child to a few of the other students at a time. Help him or her learn to pronounce the names of classmates, and have them practice the new child's name. Be sure to continue eye contact and gestures of reassurance throughout the day. Provide support as often as possible. Do whatever you can to make your classroom feel like a safe place for learning, for making mistakes, and for experimenting with new, more effective ways of communicating.

SELECT DISPLAY MATERIALS

By carefully planning how you use the space and place items in your room, you will be able to create an environment that supports English learners. Posting labels and incorporating multicultural displays and materials will send a message that you care about your students and want them to be successful.

Introduce Labels

To help students develop their English language skills, label items in your room with name cards. Create safety signs using pictures. Label supply closets with pictures and names of objects. Have dictionaries readily available, and use them often yourself to model for the children. Make time for the new student to teach classmates the names of things in his or her own language. In this way, there is a beginning cultural exchange, and the English learner feels valued. You will also end up introducing all your students to a world of different cultures and languages that will only make them more adaptable after they leave school.

In one classroom, the teacher took inventory of all the languages that students spoke at home, numbering close to a dozen. She then made up signs of the most common features of the room and had the students insert the names in their native languages. Next to the light switch, for example, was a sign that read "Luces," "Lumières," "Luci," "Lichter," proclaiming in Spanish, French, Italian, German, and many other tongues what was located in this spot. Not only did this give helpful directions, but it also communicated respect for the many different ways of saying the same thing.

Organize Support Materials

English learners benefit greatly from the use of visual aids. Begin early to collect samples of real objects that are mentioned in your standards and appear in your textbook. English learners may not be familiar with the objects or may not yet connect the English words to the objects. Select models of items to support your units. One high school teacher found having artifacts and pictures to show students to be extremely helpful:

> One of the first things I did as a new teacher was to begin a picture file. I collected all sorts of magazines and began to cut out pictures. Some I used on bulletin boards, others I put in file folders to distribute to students in small groups to look at and write about. A dedicated drawer in a file cabinet soon filled up.

Check with your school to see what resources are available. Set aside some space in your room to store the collected items as you build your own resource files. Local universities and museum may have educational trunks available for loan. Then, too, it's amazing what you will find at yard sales.

Use Multicultural Materials in the Classroom

By the way you design your space, you communicate to others that differences are valued. Hanging up posters reflecting the diversity of people and customs in our society sends a message to students and their parents. For example, you can display different alphabets used around the world. Pictures of people's faces from other countries can also be represented. One teacher reveals a favorite strategy:

> I always put up a map of the world and have my students indicate with a pushpin where they are from. I find even the native English speakers have come from different states and like to identify where they were born.

As this teacher implies, cultural diversity is represented not only in one's country of origin, but also in the particular geographical region where one's family might have come from. Clearly, students from Texas, New York, Hawaii, or Mississippi also speak different dialects and embrace different cultural customs.

Feature the accomplishments of people from different backgrounds. Play different kinds of music. Select posters that reflect different styles of art from around the world. Bring speakers to the classroom to talk about their cultures so that students will become familiar with a variety of customs—not only clothing and food, but also mannerisms and values. Often the students' relatives will be happy to bring artifacts from home and share their personal experiences with the class. Read stories from different cultures. Identify concepts around which to plan a multicultural curriculum for the classroom so that students will be able to view the world around them from diverse ethnic perspectives.

Finding the best reading materials for reaching students who are learning to speak, read, and write English is a challenge for teachers. Having a number of books that represent the different cultures and home languages of the students in your class can help welcome newcomers into your classroom. A small classroom library or even a single shelf on a bookcase that is devoted to multicultural literature can help students feel welcome. There are a number of professional organizations, such as the International Reading Association, National Association for Multicultural Education, the National Council for the Social Studies, and the National Council of Teachers of English, that provide lists of high-quality multicultural literature.

Display Student Work

Save a place on your bulletin board to put up examples of student work. Nothing shows the evidence of a learning community like a display of students' accomplishments (Houk, 2005). Carefully select examples so as to include work from each child. Demonstrate for students how to show respect for the work.

You can plan with your students to change your bulletin boards periodically. This approach will give your students a sense of ownership as they choose pieces that demonstrate their learning. They and their families will take pride in seeing their work in public spaces and be able to see their progress. In addition, by the end of the year, you will have turned your classroom into a museum.

ESTABLISH ROUTINES

Posting schedules and establishing regular procedures will be very helpful to all new students (Faltis & Coulter, 2007). All students benefit from knowing what each day's activities will be and what behavior is expected. It's important to inform students how you will signal that their attention is needed and how you expect them to get your attention. Then, too, teachers must remember to acknowledge their students' accomplishments.

Set Routines

Students new to North America may need to learn how to "do" school, at least according to our customs and rules. Begin by being conscious of your terminology. Use the same wording from day to day. Rather than say "It's time for gym," one day and "It's time for PE," the next, choose one term and stick with it.

Establish routines, such as how to obtain materials or how to leave the room, throughout the day and review them with the class. English learners are usually quick to follow the lead of others. With older students, you might make out a schedule for them to follow.

Consistently designating a place on your whiteboard for writing down homework assignments and important due dates can really help establish a sense of comfort for English learners. A first-year middle school teacher learned this quite early in the school year:

> Kim (a sixth grader from Vietnam) arrived in my class without knowing a single word of English. As a student with a strong foundation in her home language, she quickly picked up conversational English. However, she struggled with meeting due dates and with the daily expectations of her middle school classes. It was not until I met with her other content teachers and her ESL teacher that we realized that Kim was faced with wildly different routines and homework procedures in each of her classes. Once we realized this, we were able to establish a consistent process of writing down assignments and due dates on the left-hand side of the front boards in our classrooms, thus solving this point of confusion for Kim. (As a side note, establishing a set of common procedures for homework and due dates helped all of our students!)

CREATE A COMMUNITY OF LEARNERS

In order to maximize learning in the classroom and to encourage students to speak using their new language skills, students must be actively involved with one another. An effective way to facilitate active learning is to develop a community of learners. Teachers can nurture a sense of community not only when they show students they care about them, but also when they let students see who they are as individuals and the kinds of interests they have outside of school.

Many teachers build community with class meetings. Held on a regular basis, when all students are present in the room, maybe once a week, class meetings address classroom or school issues that need discussion. Early in the year, you should serve as the leader, preparing an agenda and setting time limits. Later on, students can co-lead or take turns leading the meeting. All students are given the opportunity to speak, one at a time. You may decide to have a recorder take notes on the proceedings.

In democratic classrooms, students work together to determine classroom rules and consequences. Teachers create a forum for students to work together to solve problems. This allows students to feel a sense of ownership over class policies and procedures. This natural "buy-in" helps maintain a respectful and smoothly running class environment. When students feel that their voices are heard, they experience firsthand how a democratic classroom operates. These kinds of democratic experiences are vital if we expect our students to later step into their roles as productive and contributing citizens.

Treat Students With Respect

Treating students with respect is vital to maintaining a positive social climate. Nurture a sense of community in your classroom by emphasizing the concepts of fairness and equity with your students. By discussing and modeling these important concepts, you will ensure that your students will learn to appreciate them—both in your classroom and in the world.

This does not mean that you should necessarily treat all students in exactly the same way. The time and energy you devote to your students will vary according to their specific needs. The key is that you know your students as individuals. This will allow you to decide what is in each student's best interest. When making equitable and fair decisions about students, you should consider the student's past performance, what you believe to be the student's immediate progress, and what you predict is the student's long-term potential. When you make informed decisions about your students in this way, they will come to see you as a respectful teacher who is genuinely making decisions in their best interests.

Another way to ensure that you are treating students with respect is to use appropriate and neutral language (Kottler & Gallavan, 2008). For example, use terms that are inclusive, such as "police officers" and "firefighters." Doing so—in both formal and informal situations—will allow your students to see how language is used in different circumstances. Recognizing that you are a role model, use communication that is gender-neutral and culturally sensitive.

Connect With Native Language Speakers

Find out if there are other children who speak the same language, if not in your classroom then somewhere else in the school. One middle school teacher suggests:

> An effective strategy I have used with my English language learner class is checking for understanding. I use a student who understands at least some English to speak in their common language to make sure the non-English-speaking student is following the gist of the lesson and is learning new words.

These student helpers can explain procedures and answer questions the student might have. They can offer emotional support by identifying with the experiences of the new student. Furthermore, they can serve as role models. Contact bilingual adults to work with you and the student.

Among members of some cultural groups, parents and children are used to thinking of school as an extension of home. Not only would bilingual adults be delighted to help out, but they might even feel disappointed when *not* invited to participate in the educational process. In one Aboriginal school on a reservation in Northern Queensland (Australia), the principal and teachers canvassed the whole surrounding community to make sure that everyone understood that the school *belonged* to all of them; it was just as much their home as a place where their children visited. Before long, parents and other adults began visiting the classrooms. In the beginning, they came mostly as observers, and then later they were put to work according to their interests and abilities. One interesting sidelight is that there were no longer any discipline problems in the school because there was always some neighbor or family member on campus to make certain that children acted in respectful, appropriate ways. Once efforts were made to make the school familiar rather than foreign territory, the students made significant progress.

Give Recognition Where It Is Due

It is important to recognize the efforts that children make, but this is especially true for those who are struggling the most. Our attention is often so drawn to problems that we forget to notice incremental improvement, especially in those who are having the most difficulty.

It is generally a good idea to find as many ways as possible to provide support, reinforcement, and encouragement. Efforts should be made to introduce such recognition in a natural rather than a contrived way for significant achievements or contributions. There is nothing more disappointing than to realize that a teacher is rewarding you for some token gesture that did not really involve much effort.

FOSTER CLASSROOM INVOLVEMENT

In addition to strategies designed to build relationships with students and to help them develop rudimentary English skills, much can also be initiated within the classroom to make assimilation easier.

Assign a Buddy

As we mentioned previously, it is often helpful to assign students to be "buddies" or helpers. One classmate can be responsible for helping with schoolwork. Another can be responsible for guiding the student to lunch. A third can be responsible for identifying the correct bus for the ride home after school. These initial contacts often lead to friendships with young learners in which the child must learn to speak better English in order to communicate. Be advised that sometimes the buddy support ends when students leave the classroom, leaving the English learner disappointed.

In particular, a study partner will be useful in showing the student what materials to use, demonstrating procedures, and re-explaining information in "student" language. The partner can read to the child and work with the student orally until literacy skills develop. The partner will model social customs appropriate to the classroom. In return, the partner has the opportunity to develop responsibility and leadership skills. In fact, in the optimal classroom environment, children compete for the privilege of guiding the newcomer.

Small Groups

As the comfort level rises, the nature of the student's participation in the classroom can change to include cooperative groups.

The small-group setting may actually be more consistent with the child's cultural background than the whole-class setting. There is considerable evidence that small instructional groups work well with English learners (Garcia, 1991). Students from different ethnic and racial backgrounds need practice in working together. The English learner especially can benefit from cooperative learning. For students learning English, the input from a small group may well be more comprehensible than teacher-led, large-group discussion. In addition, the English learner is able to practice communication in a less threatening environment in a small group.

Small groups will give the student exposure to additional peers, provide for hearing different points of view (as well as accents), and enable him or her to contribute to a project. The student will have the opportunity to try out new language skills with peers as an audience before facing the teacher.

"I think small groups are less threatening to children," one teacher admits before continuing:

> Children often fear they will be laughed at if they make a mistake. They don't want to be ridiculed in front of a big audience. In small groups they can make contributions in various ways without needing to use a lot of language. They can be a timer, an artist, an encourager, or the supplies captain. Also, they hear "kid talk" rather than "teacher talk," which is probably the language they are more interested in learning.

In one school, a teacher adapted some of the activities from "adventure-based" interventions so that English learners were mixed with other children and then given group assignments that were essentially nonverbal—cooperating in such a way as to get everyone through an obstacle course; to take turns catching one another during "trust falls"; and to do group "juggling," in which the children work to get as many balls into play as possible.

Another popular small-group instructional strategy is the use of literature circles (Daniels, 1994, 2002). Literature circles are a powerful reading and discussion strategy that can be used with fiction or nonfiction texts at all grade levels. By combining collaborative learning and independent reading, literature circles offer students an engaging way both to read and to engage in meaningful discussions.

Literature circles are small, peer-led discussion groups whose members have all chosen to read the same book, chapter, article, or novel. Harvey Daniels (2002) describes 11 key ingredients to literature circles, but in our minds the essence of this strategy can be summed up as follows: (1) Students choose their reading materials; (2) Groups meet on a regular basis to discuss the readings; (3) The small-group discussions are student-generated rather than teacher-directed; (4) Students each have different, yet equally important roles to play in the small-group discussions; (5) A sense of enjoyment permeates all that happens.

For years, many language arts and English teachers have used literature circles, but recently, literature circles have been used with informational texts as well (Daniels, 2002). MacGillivray (1995) suggests that literature circles are an excellent tool to use with English learners. They can pair with a buddy to read or listen to a book on tape (Houk, 2005). As will become more evident in Chapter 3, where we explore second language acquisition in more depth, literature circles tap into many of the basic principles of second language acquisition, so it is not surprising that they are a popular strategy among teachers of English learners. Houk (2005) suggests teaming with a teacher from another subject area to create a thematic unit.

Whole Group

Following individual conversations with you and practice with partners or small groups of students, the English learners should be ready to speak in front of the entire class. You may decide to deliberately prepare the learner to answer one particular question at a future time: "Okay, Miguel, tomorrow during math I am going to ask for a volunteer to tell us what is most similar between two different sets of numbers. Now, what are you going to say?"

In order to build confidence and skills incrementally, it is often helpful to conduct such rehearsals with children who are particularly anxious or hesitant. If time permits, you can even role-play situations that are predicted to occur next. For instance, "Nadya, when you go to the cafeteria next hour and stand in line for lunch, let's say that instead of pointing to what you want to order, you ask for it. How will you say what you want? Pretend I am the person standing behind the counter."

Structured Responses

Learning English as an acquired language takes a long time. Students will be able to understand long before they are able to speak. There may be a silent period in which the student learns by listening but is not ready to talk. The learning will be facilitated by your conscious incorporation of strategies, such as use of gestures, visual aids, realia, and repetition. In response, the student can demonstrate comprehension by using gestures or pointing to pictures. You can also ask students to "act out" a response to a question. We will present teaching strategies in depth in later chapters.

For many children, speaking in front of a group of people—especially one including an adult in a position of authority—can be a terrifying experience. Carefully wording questions to call for a "yes" or "no" response, or providing a choice of words for the student to choose from, will make it easier for a student just beginning to learn English. Later, open-ended questions can generate more extensive answers. It's important to give students a reason for talking. When students are excited about a topic, they will engage.

As mentioned previously, students can practice with partners or in a small group before giving a response in front of the entire class. It is vitally important to extend your *wait time*, that is, the amount of time you allow a student to formulate and give a response. English learners often need just a little more time. Your patience and your students' patience will be appreciated. Chapter 3 will discuss the stages of language acquisition and what kinds of responses you as a teacher can expect.

CELEBRATE DIVERSITY

As mentioned above, by selecting and displaying materials featuring people from around the world you will be celebrating diversity. Another way is to support the diversity of your English learners by viewing them as a resource in your classroom.

One teacher is continually reminded of the importance of valuing students as individuals:

> While waiting in line at a football game I was surprised by a gentle tap on the back, followed by a tentative question: "Is that you, Mr. S?" As I turned to meet the voice behind me I was greeted by Hugo, a student I had not seen since he left my sixth-grade class, over 15 years ago. We stopped to chat for a few minutes and I discovered that Hugo was now an engineer, having graduated from a well-regarded university. But what impressed me most about seeing Hugo again was his acknowledgment that I had made him feel important in sixth grade. He recalled how I greeted him by name as he entered the class each morning, how I read his journal entries aloud as examples of descriptive writing, and how I showed patience as he struggled to develop as an academic writer. Now an adult, he told me how significant it was to have had a teacher who acknowledged him as a valuable resource in the classroom.

Teachers of English learners should include discussions that call for different points of view in their lesson planning (Tomlinson & McTighe, 2006). When teachers create a safe and respectful community of learners, students will develop the confidence to present differing cultural perspectives on any number of topics. As a result they will increase their appreciation of commonalities and differences and expand their thinking.

Students can also share the knowledge, skills, and dispositions they have developed from their previous school experiences, as well as their personal experiences. Invite them to tell their stories, explain their understanding and insights, give examples, and/or model their skills. You never know what expertise is sitting in your room. Teachers can help students be proud of who they are as individuals and proud of their cultures as they learn about their new community. Create an environment that is welcoming for students, regardless of their English proficiency levels (see Box 2.1).

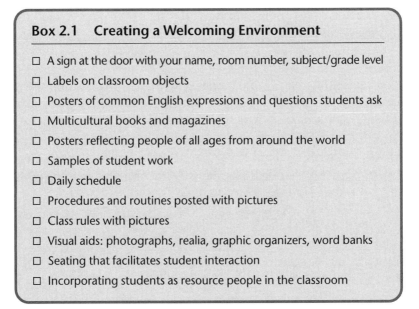

Box 2.1   Creating a Welcoming Environment

☐ A sign at the door with your name, room number, subject/grade level

☐ Labels on classroom objects

☐ Posters of common English expressions and questions students ask

☐ Multicultural books and magazines

☐ Posters reflecting people of all ages from around the world

☐ Samples of student work

☐ Daily schedule

☐ Procedures and routines posted with pictures

☐ Class rules with pictures

☐ Visual aids: photographs, realia, graphic organizers, word banks

☐ Seating that facilitates student interaction

☐ Incorporating students as resource people in the classroom

OPEN DOORS TO FAMILIES

Whether you work with elementary or secondary students, families play an important role in the education of your students. There are many types of families, and they operate in different ways. Some you will see often, others rarely. Some will be active participants, others silent supporters, and a few may be passive observers. Opening doors to parents and families is the first step to creating partnerships for supporting student success in school.

Meeting the Families

Getting to know students means knowing their families. All behavior occurs not only within a cultural context but also within a unique family environment. Based on what is called "systems theory," teachers are encouraged to look at all individual behavior within a much larger perspective. If a student is having trouble in school, these problems may very well be the result of things going on at home. Likewise, the child's behavior influences the actions of others within the family. Because the classroom and school are also human systems, the same thing is true there as well: each person's behavior is both the cause and effect of the behavior of others within the community.

It is for this reason that some teachers and many counselors are inclined to think in "systemic" terms whenever they encounter difficulties, asking questions such as the following:

1. What is this student's behavior really saying?

2. Who is the student possibly helping or enabling as a result of maintaining the status quo?

3. What would be the influence and impact of change for this student?

4. What "benefits" is this student enjoying as a result of remaining stuck?

5. What is the particular meaning of this behavior in light of the student's family history and current situation?

Imagine, for example, that a student whom you know is quite bright and capable makes only meager progress in learning and applying English proficiency in school. Because the student already speaks fluent French in addition to several different dialects of her native country, you know she is quite capable in language development, yet for some reason she does not seem to be learning—or at least using—much English in her daily interactions.

Upon investigating further, you discover that her parents are having relationship problems at home, threatening divorce. As long as their child is struggling in school, the parents are remaining together for the sake of family stability. In their culture, doing well in school is the only measure of success in their new country. That their child is doing so poorly is a source of great shame and anguish to all of them, but ironically, it is the glue that is keeping the family intact. The consequences of the child improving significantly might very well be the parents splitting up, so the child is actually functioning as a stabilizing factor.

It is often extremely important to build bridges with families and parents so as to better understand the larger context for the student's behavior as well as to structure interventions that involve the whole family. After all, it is one of teachers' greatest sources of frustration that we can do our jobs so well in school, and then everything can be undone once the students leave our influence. This is especially the case if children live in communities or homes that directly or indirectly sabotage school performance.

There will be several occasions for meeting with the parents of your students—open house at school; parent conferences; and other school events, such as field days, recitals, and awards ceremonies. Besides participating in required school activities, you will benefit from attending other school programs where parents will be in attendance, whether it is a school meeting for parents, a concert, or an athletic event. Or, better yet, attend community events where you may see students and their families in other roles.

Generally speaking, it is a principle of systemic intervention that the more participants you get involved in the change process, the more likely you are to influence the whole system in an enduring way. This could very well mean that with some "parent" conferences it might be entirely appropriate to invite grandparents and other extended family members as well.

Opening Lines of Communication

To prepare for the school encounters, you can send explanatory letters home, provided they are in the parents' native language and the parents can read. Reach out to parents through bilingual school staff and through translators and interpreters in written and oral communications, respectively (Houk, 2005). A telephone call from someone who speaks the native language will also acquaint the parents with the customs of the school. Some parents will not be able to come to school if there are younger children in the home. You will have to inform them if baby-sitting is available or if they will be welcome to bring the younger children with them. Transportation may also be a problem. Arranging for rides with a neighbor or a parent volunteer would be helpful.

Be aware that to parents from some cultures, a letter or call from school can be a source of embarrassment. These parents feel it is their responsibility to teach their children how to behave. Any request from the school may be misinterpreted as a failure on their part. Such situations can be avoided if the teacher, or another parent, can explain the importance of parent-teacher communication and the school emphasis on involving parents in the educational process through regular conferences.

Sometimes though, parents may not feel capable of communicating with the schools. This was the case for many Mexican American families in one community (Delgado-Gaitan, 1993). To combat this problem, the parents began meeting regularly, eventually organizing a parent group through which to better communicate their needs and desires to the school personnel. These parents were truly passionate in their desire to support their children, but they did not have the means to do so until the parent group was formed. Once this happened, communication with the school improved, despite language and cultural issues that had prohibited clear communication in the past. You may be able to facilitate a meeting of the parents of your students.

Parent Conferences

There are several things to keep in mind when conducting parent conferences (see Kottler & Kottler, 2007; Lawrence & Hunter, 1995). Greeting the parents by name with the correct pronunciation will make a positive first impression. Allow plenty of time. Let the parents look around the room and familiarize themselves with the setting. Inform the parents that conferences are requested on a regular basis as school policy. Encourage the parents to talk about their child by asking questions:

- What is the child's behavior like at home?
- What were the child's past educational experiences like?
- Does the child mention any problems or difficult situations?
- Is the child or any other member of the family experiencing any cultural conflicts?
- What are the parents' or guardians' goals for the child with respect to education?
- Are there any special needs or customs you need to take into consideration?

If the parent or guardian is not able to communicate, a family member or friend can help mediate the conversation. Or, request that an interpreter be present for the conference.

Parents may not be familiar with grading scales and testing measures. Therefore, reports that have been sent home from school may be ignored or misinterpreted. Much attention has been placed on testing of late, and it will be helpful to explain the purpose and importance of the criterion-based and norm-referenced tests particular to your school district. You may also want to present the importance of homework as a supplement to class instruction to the parents.

One way in which schools in the United States differ from schools in other parts of the world is in extracurricular activities. From clubs and enrichment classes in art, dance, and music to athletics, native English-speaking children have many choices of activities from the time they leave school in the afternoon through the early evening. It is important to explain the significance of these activities to all parents, as they are not all available to all children as part of their school curriculum.

Today, many districts offer free afterschool tutoring and enrichment programs. Schools may be open as late as 6:00 p.m., offering a variety of activities from jewelry making to bicycle repair, as well as additional individual educational support. They provide nutritious snacks for the students. Late transportation home may be available as well. These programs offer a safe and nurturing environment in which English language development will be enhanced.

Parents will have different assumptions about the role of the teacher in their child's education. For example, some parents often expect a formal atmosphere and strict discipline in the classroom. They see the teacher as the authority and therefore may not understand the purpose of such activities as learning centers and writing workshops until these are explained. Rote memorization and observation are activities with which they are familiar. They would expect emphasis on the basics, and they will be uncomfortable making decisions about their child's welfare, being accustomed to deferring to the professional educator. Rather than viewing these parents as uncaring, a teacher who is familiar with the values of the family will be able to see such responses as respectful or deferential and avoid misinterpretation.

It is also helpful to collect samples of the student's work to present to the parents to show their child's progress. Pictures of the student involved in various activities will also provide information to parents about how time in school is spent. You can involve the student in the conference to explain, in the language the parents best understand, the accomplishments made up to this point, how the student is evaluated, and goals identified for the future.

By developing your sensitivity to the socially appropriate customs related to interpersonal relations of the home culture, you will begin to build bridges that will further aid the work you are doing with the children. You will be able to recruit parents as partners in developing mutually agreed-on goals for the students.

Teaching is about developing relationships with children, regardless of the way communication is initiated. The better you get to know the English learner, the more able you are to relate to him or her in language that is accessible. You will be able to find meaningful ways to connect your subject to the learner as you make your class relevant to the child's background and interests. What greater gift can we offer children than the opportunity to improve their ability to express themselves?

SUGGESTED ACTIVITIES

1. Reflect on (or discuss in class or small groups) those factors that made classrooms most and least comfortable for you. What did teachers do that made you feel most likely to become actively involved? What did teachers do that inhibited you most?

2. Create labels in English for materials and supplies in your classroom. Then identify the routines you would like your students to follow. Practice these routines with all students.

3. Brainstorm ways to create a multicultural environment in the classroom. Identify multicultural books that would be of interest to your students. Share this list with them and see if they or their family members have any titles to add.

4. Develop a number of activities that you could use in your classroom appropriate for (a) paired, (b) small-group, and (c) whole-group lessons.

5. Role-play parent conferences representing several of the cultural groups that you are most likely to encounter in your classroom.

CHAPTER THREE

Understanding Second-Language Development

In order to use many of the methods presented in the previous and subsequent chapters, it is necessary to have some background in the nature of language acquisition. At the very least, you must have some notion about how children develop second-language abilities. In addition, you will need to have some idea about how long this process usually takes and what you can do to help facilitate language acquisition.

With English learners who are placed in your classroom for all or part of the day, your task becomes twofold: to teach the curriculum required by your school district and to provide language instruction in English. By becoming aware of the principles related to second-language development, you will be able to plan for the integration of content and language skills so that your students will learn to use English as they interact with each other and become involved in the academic experiences you structure for them.

SECOND-LANGUAGE PRINCIPLES

There are a number of principles that operate in the process of learning a second language. Many of these, such as the contextual nature of words—how their meaning depends on the specific situation—are a part of what teachers already understand. For example, a *party* can refer to a political group organized to promote a political platform and support its candidates, not only to a festive occasion where one eats cake and ice cream. However, other principles that emphasize social and cultural factors are not so readily apparent without some review of the underlying concepts.

Language Learning and Language Acquisition

There is a difference between learning a language and acquiring one (Krashen, 1996). The latter occurs informally as children subconsciously develop language skills by listening to others and becoming aware of language in their surroundings. This "inside-out" process takes place as students participate in their environment.

Language development also occurs in formal settings, such as when people consciously develop language skills by attending school, listening to tapes, or hiring private tutors. This "outside-in" process takes place in structured situations and, as we well know, is considerably less inspiring as an environment for developing fluency.

Because the object of language is meaningful communication, the emphasis today on teaching English to speakers of other languages is to promote second-language development in settings in which students will *acquire* the target language. As such, the goal is to provide social interactions for students in which they will create meaningful communication in English as they develop academically.

As one example, you may recall situations in a strange place in which you absolutely had to communicate in order to find a bathroom or get directions back to your hotel. Under these desperate circumstances, we are often amazed at how quickly we can acquire the necessary verbal (and nonverbal) skills to get our needs met. The object of our educational efforts is to structure just such situations for students, in which they acquire English as a means for survival or in a way that is useful in accomplishing a task, rather than as another in a series of homework assignments.

Developing Vocabulary

Understanding how students *acquire* new vocabulary words may also help to explain the distinction between *acquiring* new words and *learning* them. Broadly defined, vocabulary is knowledge of words and word meanings. Word knowledge comes in two forms, receptive and productive. *Receptive vocabulary* includes words that we recognize when we hear or see them. *Productive vocabulary* includes words that we use when we speak or write. Because many English learners may not read very much in English, they often don't have the opportunity to see and learn very many new English words. This is unfortunate, because when good readers read more, they become better readers, and learn more words.

There is considerable agreement among researchers that all students add approximately 2,000 to 3,500 distinct words to their reading vocabularies each year. Yet how is this possible, since to directly teach students even 3,000 words a year would mean teaching approximately 17 words each school day (e.g., 3,000 words divided by 180 school days)? The answer is *incidental learning*—that is, through exposure to and interaction with increasingly complex and rich oral language and by encountering lots of new words in text, either through their own reading or by being read to (National Institute of Child Health and Human Development, 2000).

Developing understandings of word meanings is a long-term process, and involves many encounters with both spoken and written words in varying contexts. For example, when a student first encounters a new word, some information about that word is stored in memory, yet the student by no means "owns" that word. Upon seeing this word over and over—in multiple contexts—the student picks up more information about the word from its use in various settings. Over time, the student acquires many pieces of information about that word. As a result, the student gradually acquires "ownership" of the word.

Teachers who provide students with multiple instructional contexts for learning new words will best enable their students to acquire rich vocabularies. English learners need to encounter key vocabulary words (words that likely appear in many contexts) often. The words are integrated into everyday classroom experiences, and students are provided opportunities to use the words in meaningful ways relating to or applying the content (e.g., not just writing the words 10 times each).

To help students to acquire new words quickly, keep the following acronym in mind: RIM (Repetition, Integration, and Meaningful Context):

- **R—Repetition.** Multiple exposures to vocabulary items are crucial if we want students to eventually "own" these words. Students should be presented with words that will likely appear in many contexts.
- **I—Integration.** Using the words in multiple contexts is easy to accomplish. For example, use key vocabulary in your daily lessons, create word walls to reinforce these words, and encourage students to use the words in their daily conversations. By integrating the vocabulary into your classroom structures, you are allowing students to acquire new vocabulary as they naturally meet those words in the course of their daily lives as students.
- **M—Meaningful Context.** When vocabulary words are derived from content learning materials, the learner will be better equipped to deal with specific reading matter in content areas. Also, when English learners view acquiring new vocabulary as important to them personally, they are more likely to pick up those new words than if they are simply presented with a list of terms that they need to master.

Appropriate Level of Communication

In order to foster development of English, you as the teacher must provide communication that can be understood. This should include words that students already understand, along with new vocabulary that they will be able to figure out from the context in which it is presented. If the student is able to understand what you are trying to communicate, then you have created what Krashen (1996) refers to as *comprehensible input*. For example, a teacher addresses a child as follows: "Maria, I [points to self]—want—you [points to child]—to listen [points to ear]." When the teacher has evidence that Maria understands each of these words so far, she continues, "Please, stand up [gestures with hands and then demonstrates]." Consequently, the teacher must pay attention to (a) delivery—for example, making sure to pronounce words clearly and using real objects and gestures; (b) content—making sure material is appropriate and familiar; and (c) environment—creating a comfortable atmosphere in which students have positive experiences that are relatively free of anxiety.

Systems of Language

When a person is learning English, he or she is learning not only the sounds of the language (phonology), how words are built (morphology), the meanings of the sounds (semantics), and the rules that govern the structure of the language (syntax), but also the particular situations in which these words would be used. The person also needs to know the social context—when and how to use it. Distinguishing when to use formal and informal expressions is as important as knowing grammatical rules and vocabulary words. For example, one would not use the expression "Wazzup?" (What's up?) in addressing a judge in a courtroom; however, it would be appropriate for saying hello to a friend passing by on a city street.

Students will acquire the language systems by listening to and observing other people, as well as by explanations. It is important to carefully plan lessons that involve students in speaking and writing activities with one another so they will have opportunities to develop purposeful expressions and increase their language ability. They will realize that there is a difference in how one responds depending on whether it is a formal or informal interaction. The language they use with you, the teacher, will be different from the language they use with peers, such as in the cafeteria or on the playground.

LANGUAGE PROCESSES

There are four areas of language proficiency. The two related to oral performance are listening and speaking, with the component parts of pronunciation, grammar, and vocabulary. It is in these areas that students first develop mastery. There is ready stimulation and much social—not to mention survival—motivation to understand speech, to carry on a conversation, and to be able to ask questions. However, it must be noted that for most people who are learning a second language, there is a silent period that takes place. As students become accustomed to the sounds and meanings of sounds and symbols, they will be in a receptive rather than an initiating mode of behavior. They will speak little, if at all, in the beginning. Remember, this does not mean they are not learning—they are just processing what they hear.

The two areas related to written performance include the ability to read and write. The corresponding component parts are spelling, grammar, and vocabulary. As you have no doubt noticed, these areas take longer to develop. Students who lack proficiency in these areas have trouble in classes that focus on reading, such as history and literature courses. Given that it may take students up to 15,000 hours of exposure to learn a language, teachers must be very patient.

Content-Based Approach

Current research in language development calls for simultaneous development, fostering a balanced language experience without fragmenting the systems into discrete parts. The current school of thought is to teach English using a content-based approach, that is, through subject areas rather than with a focus on grammar. This is precisely the situation faced by the regular classroom teacher. As students are involved in meaningful learning activities that stimulate them on a cognitive level, they will develop the corresponding necessary English language skills. For example, as you introduce a unit on nutrition, the students will learn the terminology and expressions associated with food and health habits that contribute to daily life.

Achieving Competence

A student first develops simple conversational skills. Freeman and Freeman (1998) describe the results of James Cummins' (1981, 1996) research in language acquisition. Conversational language, which Cummins referred to as developing basic interpersonal communicative skills (BICS) in a second language, often takes one to two years. These skills of social communication are related to the settings in which they occur (school, neighborhood, store). They are characterized as contextual, in that the student gains meaning from clues in the situation—objects, pictures, gestures, and other aspects of nonverbal communication. Within two years, a student can often participate in face-to-face conversation that is concrete and cognitively undemanding.

Often, when verbal fluency is developed, people assume that the student can perform equally well in reading and writing tasks. A high school teacher explains:

> A Mexican teenager of my acquaintance moved to this country from Mexico City with his two older brothers. He attended high school for a while and then dropped out. I was surprised by his academic difficulties, given that he was verbally expressive. When I asked him why he dropped out of school, he replied matter-of-factly that it was because he couldn't read the textbooks in English.

It may take five to seven years for a student to develop cognitive academic language proficiency (CALP), which requires literacy. This proficiency is characterized by the ability to understand academic language, which is often abstract, and the ability to function at an advanced cognitive level. Synthesizing information from different sources is an example of CALP.

Therefore, don't be surprised when children placed in regular classrooms are able to converse well and get along with their fellow students, but have trouble mastering the content you present and so receive failing grades on tests. Their reading and writing skills may fall well below the level required for success. They may also lack the cultural experiences needed to achieve immediate success in the classroom and on standardized tests. As teachers, we need to develop activities in which all students can participate and demonstrate achievement. This chapter presents many ideas for your consideration.

DEVELOPING PROFICIENCY

As you well know, learning varies from one individual to the next. In this section, we will look at the factors that affect how children learn during the stages of development as well as assessments used in schools.

Learning Rates

As with anything else about human behavior, there are vast individual differences in learning rates (Harper & de Jong, 2004). Of the social and cultural factors that play a part, none should be taken in isolation.

- For some children, learning English will come easily and effortlessly. It is a goal they eagerly work toward. They will have support at home from their parents.

- For others, learning English may create serious problems as they are caught between two cultures that emphasize different values. Such students may feel torn between the demands of home versus those at school.

- Many students undergo extreme socioeconomic changes when they come to North America. As people move from rural to urban areas or from middle-class to lower-class status, the families face internal adjustment even before language becomes an issue. Regardless of status, culture shock is likely to exert some influence, especially during the first year.

- Some form of racial and ethnic discrimination is a reality of life for many students acquiring English. Many people who are already citizens here feel that new immigrants threaten the economic and social stability of our country. The impact of prejudice and discrimination leads to low self-esteem in students. They feel that less is expected of them, and this is often the case. Their perceptions of themselves will affect their school performance. As teachers, we need to be sensitive to and minimize such practices.

- Age makes a difference, too. Research has substantiated a phenomenon that most people have already observed: Children of certain ages can pick up another language faster than people at other ages. In fact, some studies show that children between the ages of 8 and 12 acquire a second language faster than children between the ages of 4 and 7 and those older than 12. Thus adolescents especially may be subjected to risky situations when they are placed in the regular classroom. They are expected to do grade-level academic work and are graded accordingly when they have not achieved proficiency in English. There is also great discussion on the appropriateness of requiring English learners to take standardized tests and high-stakes/proficiency tests when they are not fluent in English.

- Change in teaching styles. Many students come from countries that are highly teacher-centered rather than student-centered. Students used to classes of lecture, note-taking, and memorization need time to adjust to student-centered classes where they are asked to be actively involved in discussion using critical thinking skills, such as in inquiry-based learning or project-based learning.

Proficiency Levels

Language development is usually divided into several levels of increasing complexity. School districts vary in the number of levels they use to determine the proficiency of students. In one sample district (Clark County, Nevada), the following stages are delineated:

1. Preproduction Stage

At this level, very basic communication, if any, can be expected, with simple oral and written responses. Students may be hesitant to speak and tend to use a lot of nonverbal communication, such as pantomime, pointing to objects, and nodding the head to indicate "yes" or "no" in response to questions. Such individuals can show agreement or disagreement with "thumbs up" and "thumbs down" gestures. Another technique is to provide students with numbered sticks, then ask them a multiple-choice question and have them hold up the number that corresponds to their answer. Students can also draw pictures to demonstrate understanding and are comfortable matching words to pictures or objects.

At this beginning stage, teachers—and other students—need to do a lot of modeling for beginning students. Students will rely heavily on the teacher's body language, so gestures play a key role in developing understanding. It is important to use as many visual references as possible with pictures and artifacts. Providing opportunities for lessons that use art and music will be critical.

2. Early Production Stage

At the advanced beginning level, students add extended vocabulary and more complex grammar and focus on more complex reading and writing skills. Comprehension increases, and students begin to speak. Students will be able to identify people and objects. They may understand the main idea of a presentation or a story but will not be able to understand each word or phrase. Students will be able to do short sentence-completion tasks. They will be able to repeat common expressions and begin to use common phrases on their own. There may be some mispronunciation as they begin to develop speaking skills, but there is no need to make corrections unless the meaning is unclear. Teachers can begin to ask simple yes-or-no, who, what, where, when, and why questions. The introduction of new vocabulary is important. "Think alouds" are helpful strategies for students. Rich learning environments that stimulate all the senses are needed.

3. Speech-Emergent Stage

At the beginning intermediate level, students begin to use descriptive terms in relating events. Pronunciation and intonation improve. Vocabulary increases. Students begin to initiate conversation. Comparisons and contrasts can be accomplished, as students can handle academic concepts. Students are able to categorize and summarize information.

Teachers can ask open-ended questions and encourage students to respond. Support material in the form of visual aids and graphic organizers continues to be important. It remains important for teachers to model, reinforce, and emphasize student language.

4. Intermediate Fluency Stage

Student comprehension has improved considerably. At this stage, students speak with few grammatical errors. They are able to share experiences, generate ideas, and give opinions. They begin to think in English rather than translate from their native language. Their language skills include debating, persuading, and negotiating with others. They can demonstrate higher-order thinking skills of synthesis, analysis, and evaluation.

Teachers need to provide opportunities for student interaction. Cooperative learning groups enable students to work on a task where speech is needed, but correct grammar is not crucial. Teachers can provide more complex academic work. Students can make use of print and online reference material to create projects. Teachers can introduce colloquialisms and idiomatic expressions.

Providing opportunities to publish student work or give presentations will motivate students.

5. Fluency Stage

At this level students have near-perfect speech. They have no trouble interacting with native English speakers, and read English with high levels of comprehension. Students may need help understanding abstract concepts. They continue to learn new vocabulary. Their reading and writing abilities will be comparable to that of students their age who are native English speakers.

Teachers can expect students to give oral presentations, engage in role-play situations, and debate ideas. They can complete research projects with full reports. Support may be needed for abstract ideas. Providing sheltered English and cooperative learning strategies will continue to be important.

At the highest levels, students apply language skills to increasingly abstract thought as well as to highly technical material. Students continue vocabulary and grammar development as oral and written communication skills are further strengthened.

These stages are consistent with the work of Stephen Krashen and Tracy Terrell (1983), which identified stages of language production and showed that teachers can promote students' responses by providing appropriate input, waiting for students to be ready to speak and write, and allow errors as long as they do not interfere with communication in a positive environment. Hill and Flynn (2006) point out that with careful prompting teachers can facilitate progress as students use the proficiency they have developed and move into the next level.

ASSESSING FLUENCY LEVELS

Most school districts use a battery of standardized tests, such as the CTB/McGraw-Hill Language Assessment Scales (LAS) developed by Sharon E. Duncan and Edward A. De Avila. The LAS Reading/Writing, for example, is available at three levels: Grades 2–3, Grades 4–6, and Grades 7–9+. The test items include vocabulary (synonyms and antonyms, language fluency, reading for information, mechanics, and usage) and ask students to do a writing sample. There are two forms available at each level for pre-post purposes, used with the LAS Oral to determine levels of listening, speaking, reading, and writing. The LAS were developed to measure English language proficiency and are used to classify and place limited-English students in classes. The Pre LAS is for younger children in preschool, kindergarten, and first grade. If your students have been assessed and you have access to their records, their scores will give you an indication of their skills.

A second test is the Idea Proficiency Test, which also measures vocabulary, pronunciation, syntax, and functional use of language. Students are asked to distinguish between minimal pairs, identify objects, listen to a story, and answer questions.

Another common test is the Bilingual Syntax Measure, in which students are shown cartoonlike pictures and are asked to respond to questions. This test measures whether students respond appropriately based on their grammatical expressions. It does not measure reading and writing ability. It is used to place students in classes.

There are other commercial tests as well. Many states have now developed their own assessments, such as the English Language Proficiency Assessment (ELPA) in Nevada, the California English Language Development Test (CELDT) in California, or the New York State English as a Second Language Achievement Test (NYSESLAT).

A warning: The tests are often given when students first come to school, a time that can be overwhelming as they try to make sense of the new environment. Taking a placement test may create additional anxiety. The purpose of the test may not be clear; therefore, students may not understand the importance of the test. Also, the items on the test may not have any meaning for the students, so the scores may not give a true picture of students' capabilities. Use the information that is helpful, but remember that assessment needs to be an ongoing activity.

Most classroom teachers begin with assessing oral proficiency by talking to students and noticing responses. Your personal observations of behavior will also provide information on your students. You can take notes on conversations, or record conversations and listen to them later to evaluate oral language development. These observations can be compared with your state framework or a commercially prepared checklist (Houk, 2005). Although this method is more time consuming, the data can be used immediately in planning.

HIGH-STAKES TESTING

One of the greatest challenges for children who are English learners, even those who are fluent, is taking standardized tests. As states are adopting and implementing standards, they are incorporating assessments for high-stakes testing. Olson (2001) reports that the American Educational Research Association and the National Research Council support the Standards for Educational and Psychological Testing conclusion that high-stakes decisions, such as those for promotion or graduation, should not be based on a single test. However, what other demonstrations of student achievement—such as course grades and portfolios—should be included have not yet been established.

It is interesting to note that states are taking different approaches to high-stakes testing, such as proficiency tests linked with high school diplomas. Some districts are taking into account multiple measures, such as substitution of end-of-course exams. There is much variation from state to state. Olson (2001) describes the alternative New Jersey offers for its students. This state has a series of open-ended tasks that students do during the school year, called the Special Review Assessment. Indiana offers a waiver process to students who fail. Discussion on how to assess students will continue in the future.

With the passage of the No Child Left Behind (NCLB) legislation in 2001, high-stakes testing became of crucial importance to educators of English learners. The NCLB Act of 2001 established the following goals related to English learners:

- All students, including English learners, will attain "proficiency" in mathematics by 2014.
- All English learners will become proficient in English.

Schools are accountable for improvements each year in both English learner academic (reading and mathematics) performance and English proficiency. The act mandates annual English proficiency testing, interventions for failing schools, monitoring and reporting of English learner performance on English proficiency and academic standards, and reporting of dropout and graduation rates of English learners. Under the act's firm accountability provisions, states must describe how they will close the achievement gap and make sure that all students—regardless of English proficiency—achieve academic proficiency. With high-stakes testing, schools will need to adhere to strict state and federal accountability standards—even as some students arrive with limited English proficiency skills.

FIRST- TO SECOND-LANGUAGE LEARNING

Positive Transfer

Students will not be learning English independent of their first language. Some skills developed in the student's native language will transfer to English. For this reason, there is strong support for bilingual education, which allows students to continue cognitive development in their first language while learning English at the same time.

Positive transfer from one's native language to English takes many forms. Students who can read in one language know that the reason for reading is to acquire meaning. Students know that print is speech in written form. English learners have already developed concepts in their native language and have given them names. These concepts do not have to be relearned in English; they merely need English labels. Such students have a foundation on which to build; they will look for the rules underlying the English language. Many will have developed the appropriate spatial orientation—reading from left to right and from top to bottom. Some will be familiar with the letters of the alphabet; others will have to be introduced to new symbols used in reading and writing. Reading comprehension skills—such as sequencing, inferring, and drawing conclusions—will transfer to English.

Cognates

There may be *cognates*, or words that are similar because they are derived from the same origin, that the student will be able to recognize in English. Some words, such as *color*, *radio*, and *terrible*, are spelled alike in Spanish and English, although they are pronounced differently. Other words may have different spellings but will still be recognized, such as *excellent* (*excelente*) and *dentist* (*dentista*). The cognates quickly widen the student's vocabulary.

One student, who had previously been quite frustrated with her progress in learning English, had a major breakthrough when she recognized the number of English words that end in *tion*. She started rattling off a list of examples she had recently heard—sta*tion*, men*tion*, selec*tion*, func*tion*—giggling all the while. Finally, she recognized an underlying order to this "crazy language" when she was able to associate the ending with her native *cion*, as in selec*cion* or fun*cion*.

Similarly, listening skills transfer from a first to a second language. Students will be sensitive to repetitious sounds and patterns in the language. They may need help with pronunciation and syntax, however, when they are ready to speak.

By pointing out the attributes of the student's first language that transfer to English, you can help the student feel less overwhelmed. This will also help him or her develop a positive attitude toward learning.

Negative Transfer

Students will also run into situations in which previous language learning will interfere with learning English. Teachers can make students aware of such instances of negative transfer. Common mistakes in pronunciation occur when students assume a letter in their native language makes the same sound in English. The *i* in English is pronounced as the word *eye* and not as the letter *e*, which is its sound in Spanish. Grammatical rules in the native language may not apply in English—such as the double negative. False cognates—words that appear to have similar meanings but don't—can cause students to make mistakes. *Assist* does not mean "to attend," as in Spanish, but "to help." With practice, the students will avoid these mistakes. Teachers can make lists of these words that might cause confusion for students.

Errors

Mistakes are to be expected. Unless the error interferes with communication, the best way to proceed is to use the correct form in your response. It is more effective to rephrase and model the appropriate expression than to correct it. Emphasizing parts of speech and grammar drills is not an effective use of time.

Despite changing conceptions of language and new knowledge of how English learners develop their language skills, prescriptive notions of language still flourish in many classrooms today. This is especially relevant when it comes to student writing. Once students see marks emphasizing the formal features of the paper, they quite naturally come to see that what matters in school-based writing is not what they say but how they say it. The commonly accepted practice of emphasizing the formal features of language holds that grammar worksheets, spelling tests, and punctuation rules can develop these skills. However, a long tradition of research has certainly shown that methods of teaching focusing on grammar instruction are suspect (Andrews et al., 2006; Bamberg, 1978; Krashen, 1984; Mayher, 1970).

Even when students have mastered elements presented in formal instruction, they are not able to use them fluently in real communication situations inside or outside the classroom. Those who learned Spanish back in the 1960s and 1970s with the audiolingual method can tell you today, "Pablo está bien pero Luisa tiene catarro." (Pablo is fine, but Luisa has a cold.) But no one has ever asked any of us how Pablo and Luisa are doing! Language cannot be isolated into bits and pieces. The best advice comes from a teacher who says, "Model, model, model. The more the students can actually see and hear what is expected of them, instead of just listen to instruction, the better the students can internalize what is being taught to them."

Code-Switching

At times, students will resort to using both their native language and English, sometimes in the same sentence. This is known as *code-switching*. Sometimes speakers will forget a word or will lack the necessary vocabulary. However, code-switching can be a conscious effort on the part of the speaker for expression in the most effective way (depending on the audience) rather than an inability to use either language correctly. There can be several reasons for using both languages, such as to emphasize a point or to show a personal connection. Scarcella (1990) remarks that code-switching can be a sign of advanced proficiency in both languages.

Language development is a gradual process. By setting reasonable expectations, utilizing positive transfer when possible, and assessing development throughout the year, you will lead your students down the path to becoming proficient communicators.

Guidelines for structuring your personal means of communication, implementing practical teaching strategies, and making effective presentations follow in Chapter 4.

The Silent Period

As we mentioned previously, students developing skills in English will often go through a silent period in which they will not initiate very much speech. During this time, children will be observing and listening to communication. They watch for body language and listen for intonation, pronunciation, and register (appropriate language for the situation). They observe social rules (how to begin and end a conversation, when to raise a hand). At the same time, they are building up confidence and proficiency to speak. Some students may say very little, except for routine phrases, during this time.

The silent period can be very frustrating, especially for the teacher. This stage may last only a few weeks for younger children, but it may last longer for older children. It is difficult to know how much children understand. You will also have some students at the end of their silent period, whereas others will be in the beginning. You must have great patience in allowing the children to have the time they need to feel comfortable to speak. The more you work with English learners, the easier this will be.

It may be helpful for you to summarize what you know about the language development of the English learners in your classes. Table 3.1 provides an example of such a form.

Table 3.1   English Learners and Their Language Development

Student's Name	Home Language(s)	Positive Transfer	Cognates	Level of English Proficiency	Student Characteristics/ English Language Abilities

In this chapter, we looked at language development principles, proficiency levels, assessing fluency, and first- to second-language learning. In Chapter 4, we will look at strategies for teaching English learners.

SUGGESTED ACTIVITIES

1. Interview adults who, at one time, had limited English proficiency. Find out what their experiences were like trying to learn their new language. What did teachers do that was most and least helpful to them?

2. Tape-record a conversation between you and a student learning English. Evaluate your responses. Determine whether you are modeling correct expressions or giving mini-grammar lessons to the student.

3. Make a list of the native languages of your students. Chart the similarities between the first languages and English.

4. Watch a foreign-language television station or movie. Describe how you try to figure out what is happening. List the supporting devices, such as dress, mannerisms, gestures, context, and other cues that help you figure out what might be going on. At which proficiency level are you operating?

5. Explain the difference between *acquiring* and *learning* a second language to a friend. Use examples from both second-language acquisition and from vocabulary acquisition to help make your points. Use your friend's follow-up questions to help you to sharpen the distinction between acquisition and learning in your own mind.

CHAPTER FOUR

Strategies for Teaching

The review of second-language-related principles presented in Chapter 3 offers a number of applications for your classroom. You will also find that many of the strategies you have already been shown will lend themselves quite easily to adaptation. If you are seeking practical ideas, these next chapters will provide you with ideas and guidelines as they stimulate your creativity.

MOTIVATE STUDENTS TO LEARN

Like so many other aspects of learning, motivation is often the key. Especially in the case of English learners, the challenge is not so much devising strategies for teaching but motivating students to learn the new language in the first place (Nunan, 1999; Short & Echevarria, 2004/2005). So although we include a cross-section of possible teaching strategies for working with this group of students, what you do is often less important than how you do it.

To begin, we present a number of things you can do to motivate those students who are particularly hard to reach (Burden, 2000).

1. Make Sure the Difficulty of the Work Is Matched to Ability Levels

If your assignments are too easy, students become bored and disengaged; if they are too difficult, students will become frustrated and tune out. It is between boredom and anxiety that "flow" states exist, where students are totally engaged, functioning at peak performance (Csikszentmihalyi, 1996). Materials and content must be at the students' level (Echevarria, Vogt, & Short, 2004). Finding students' strengths is especially important for older students (Bartholmew, 2007).

2. Provide Useful Structure

Include clear expectations and realistic goals. Plan for graduated steps toward success as you provide feedback along the way. Note that students need a clear focus for their English development and the content they are learning (Echevarria, Vogt, & Short, 2004; Hill & Flynn, 2006). Teachers must be clear about the enduring understandings of their lessons and how their students will be successful (Tomlinson & McTighe, 2006).

3. Captivate Student Interest

One of the most frequent complaints from all students is that what they are doing in class is not interesting or relevant to their lives. When English learners can see the clear connection between what is being taught and what they want (friends, opportunities, fun), they will be far more motivated to work even if they feel it will be difficult to learn (Bartholomew, 2007).

4. Provide Support as Needed

Monitor progress carefully. Intervene before students give up or experience failure. Arrange for individual support, such as tutoring, peer help, and parent involvement. Develop achievement plans in which goals are divided into short-term and long-term units with corresponding action guidelines (Bartholomew, 2007).

5. Show a Lot of Caring

We mention this point a lot because it is so crucial. Students want teachers who care about them (Kottler, Zehm, & Kottler, 2005). Encourage students as much as you can. Reinforce their successes. Take time to develop your relationships.

6. Reinforce Student
Effort and Provide Recognition

Research shows that by reinforcing student effort and providing recognition student achievement increases (Marzano, 2003). Teachers need to explicitly teach students the importance and consequence of effort (Hill & Flynn, 2006). Students can be encouraged to take responsibility for setting their own goals and monitoring how and under what conditions they advance toward reaching their goals. When students exceed set standards and/or achieve their goals, teachers need to recognize individual achievement with specific praise based on the accomplishments.

STRUCTURE LANGUAGE DELIVERY

What to Say and How to Say It

Needless to say, when you are talking to someone who does not understand your language very well, it is important to speak slowly and distinctly. Don't distort your words or break them into syllables—just slow your rate of speech for beginners. This will enable you to enunciate your words clearly. Adjust your rate according to the proficiency of the students (Echevarria, Vogt, & Short, 2004). Reiss (2008) has several other tips: pause between phrases to help you clearly enunciate your words; use fewer pronouns; and limit contractions.

Avoid the tendency of many native English speakers to speak louder than normal, as if the decibel level makes a difference in the other person's comprehension.

Talk about things present in the room, in the "here and now." Use props and pictures for reference. Accompany your speech with lots of gestures and actions to emphasize your meaning. Restate your message in several different ways. Ask the students questions about the points that you have made to check for comprehension. Make sure students have ample time to figure out what you have said. Extend your wait time after asking a question.

Frequent repetition is needed. After you present information, have students orally review the content in pairs. Then have them write a summary. This reiteration in a variety of formats will help with comprehension and retention. Integrating topics around a theme is another way to provide students with multiple opportunities to work with a central body of language. Elementary teachers and teams in middle schools often use a thematic approach. Ancient civilizations or rain forests are popular thematic units.

Target Your Vocabulary

Teachers are always introducing new vocabulary and concepts. Several strategies were noted in Chapter 3. Identify which words will be central to your lesson. Present the vocabulary words first, and then use them with definitions during your learning activities. Use pictures to illustrate the words. Have students develop vocabulary cards or personal dictionaries and use drawings to represent the ideas. The authors of Project CRISS (Santa, Havens, & Maycumber, 1996) suggest using a "definition map" to help students determine categories, properties, and examples of words. By reviewing with students the qualities of a definition, this approach helps to personalize new words and integrate them into their working vocabulary. The "map" includes room for comparison items and illustrations. Use the same words and terms throughout your lessons.

Students are learning the way English is used in specific subject areas (such as "table" in math), and they must also learn how to complete the academic tasks (Echevarria, Vogt, & Short, 2004). These procedures incorporate another vocabulary list of words and terms for students, such as *outline, predict, map, chart, rank, paraphrase, support, categorize, symbolize,* and *clear your desk* or *line up.* Present academic content and academic vocabulary for each lesson.

Be Aware of Problem Areas

By becoming aware of your own speech, you will be more sensitive to those who do not speak English and can offer rephrasing or an explanation as needed, according to the puzzled looks of the students or their lack of appropriate responses. Idioms and abbreviations can be particularly frustrating.

Idioms

We use many idioms in everyday speech without being aware of them. Using idiomatic expressions, such as "Cat got your tongue?" or "It's raining cats and dogs!" will leave students bewildered. One newly arrived student from Peru could not figure out what the word *pretty* meant: "I thought it meant, like beautiful, but you keep saying things like "*pretty* good." Trying to avoid idioms will have you "tripping over your tongue." Besides, if we cut out these rich turns of phrase, we will narrow our range of expression and leave our speech dull and boring.

With beginners, it is wise to avoid idiomatic expressions. Simple, straightforward speech is preferred. With intermediate students, paraphrasing will be helpful. You can use such terms as part of lessons to acquaint your students with our "colorful language."

When students are confronted with an idiomatic expression, guide them to use various strategies to determine its meaning: (a) use context clues; (b) think about the literal meaning; and (c) use their background knowledge.

Acronyms

Often our speech is peppered with abbreviations. Remember to explain the meaning each time you use one, or refer to a poster that shows the ones you use frequently. Also, you can develop a lesson on common acronyms. Do you use *PE*, *VIP*, and *ASAP* in your daily vocabulary? Have students develop a dictionary or vocabulary card file for reference.

Synonyms

Whenever appropriate, point out that different words can have the same meaning. Ask if students can think of examples in their native language to share with the class. This can lead to a general discussion on regional word usage as well. Do you *carry* people to the store (in the South) or *drive* them (in the North)? Is your car's engine under the *hood* (United States) or the *bonnet* (England and Australia)?

Homonyms

Words that have the same pronunciation but different spellings and meanings challenge most elementary and secondary students. How do you distinguish *be* and *bee*; *sea* and *see*; or *two*, *too*, and *to*? How did you learn the difference between *principle* and *principal* or *capital* and *capitol*?

Homographs

Words that are spelled the same but have different pronunciations and meanings will make reading difficult for beginners. Both meanings will need to be presented before the student begins to use the vocabulary on his or her own. Contextual clues in the reading passage will aid the student's comprehension. Common examples include *lead*, *read*, *wind*, and *tear*.

Noun Phrases

Expressions that consist of two nouns or an adjective and a noun and that combine ideas can be problematic. What is an *electrical engineer*? A train conductor who is plugged into an electric outlet? Consider a *mobile home park*. Does it change location? Students have difficulty understanding noun phrases in technical and scientific texts. These are especially difficult for Spanish speakers, for example, because of the word order.

Use Sheltered English

Freeman and Freeman (1998) point out that there are two different meanings for *sheltered instruction*. One refers to the composition of students; the other refers to delivery of content, such as math, social studies, science, and health. Some school districts use sheltered instruction as a way of grouping intermediate-proficient students in one classroom for a given subject. In that way, the children with limited English proficiency do not have to compete with the native speakers. Teachers modify the delivery of content to help students develop academically as well as develop language proficiency.

Teachers also use the technique called *sheltered English* with students in classes that contain both native and nonnative speakers. This relies heavily on the use of props, pictures, charts, and hands-on activities. Demonstrations and modeling are frequently used techniques. Teachers make sure students are able to understand what is being said by controlling vocabulary and idioms. This method involves using short, simple sentences with frequent paraphrasing and repeating. It involves all students in authentic activities, such as reading newspaper articles as part of a lesson in current events, using math manipulatives, reading a food chart, or engaging in a science experiment. It also acknowledges that students go through a silent period before voluntarily speaking. Error correction is avoided. Teachers also provide for small-group, cooperative experiences so that students have the opportunity to interact with their peers in meaningful communication as they accomplish academic tasks.

For example, in a lesson on baking a cake, you would want to have assembled all the ingredients you would need and all the utensils you would use. You might begin by showing an example of the desired end product to acquaint the students with the goal. Then, name each ingredient and let the students look, taste, and smell each item. Make sure the students can see what you do. Count out two eggs as the students watch. Describe your actions as you go along: "Now, I am cracking the eggs. Next, I will separate the white from the yolk." Present the steps of the recipe one at a time, as the students watch you model the desired behavior.

Likewise, in a science experiment, you would identify the equipment and chemicals you use by pointing to them individually and naming them: beaker, graduated cylinder, spatula, triple-beam balance. You would also describe your actions, such as measuring, pouring, stirring, observing, and recording. Indicate the states of being: solids, liquids, gases, and plasma.

SCAFFOLD (SUPPORT) INSTRUCTION

Specially Designed Academic Instruction in English (SDAIE) is one approach to teaching English learners that is common in California. This approach is also known as Sheltered Instruction or Scaffolded Instruction. SDAIE is an instructional approach in academic classes for students who can speak conversational English and have intermediate proficiency in reading and writing English. Unlike English learner classes, where the primary focus is on English language development, SDAIE methods focus on content, with English language skills being acquired through the process of students learning content.

One of the major goals of SDAIE is to make the abstract more concrete through the use of instructional scaffolds. The instruction that students receive from their content teachers is not watered down. In fact, the content is amplified rather than weakened by the scaffolds (or supports) provided by the teachers. (Scaffolds are intentional, temporary, and flexible structures designed to match students' developmental levels.)

Material is presented at grade level and instruction is augmented through the use of various strategies, including the following: gestures, contextual clues, guarded vocabulary, props, maps, visual aids, graphs, advanced organizers, realia, manipulatives, dramatization, overheads, and cooperative grouping. Likewise, assessments are modified, often through the use of alternative assessments. While native English speakers may require only a single scaffold to support their learning, English learners often benefit from additional support—with two or more scaffolds supporting student learning and different assessments.

The Sheltered Instruction Observation Protocol (SIOP) model presented by Echevarria, Vogt, & Short (2004) offers a research-based approach to lesson planning that incorporates identifying standards for learning English and content area standards. The SIOP model invites teachers to plan their lessons with the following in mind: selection and preparation of materials; building background knowledge; using comprehensible input; selecting appropriate strategies; and student interaction, practice, and application with hands-on activities and manipulatives. The model also includes a guide for lesson delivery and assessment.

Include Visual Aids

Objects, demonstrations, photographs, and pictures are vital to ensure comprehension. Students need concrete references, especially at the beginning levels of proficiency. Place vocabulary words with pictures on bulletin boards or display them on screens at the front of the room. Charts, graphs, and semantic webs will also serve the purpose of providing visual references.

Toys and tools that we take for granted might not be conventional items for English learners. They may not have experienced snow, a garlic press, a pencil sharpener, or finger paint. It will be difficult for the students to find meaning in words related to objects or ideas with which they are not familiar. Careful preparation is needed to introduce background experiences for the students. Short video segments and discussion can be integrated before you teach a lesson. It also helps if you work toward creating an atmosphere and building relationships that make it safe and comfortable for students to admit that they don't know what you mean. Consider recording a presentation or activity for playback at a later time. It can be used for reinforcement, review, or reteaching. Ideas for using technology are presented in Chapter 7.

Provide Written Support

Vocabulary lists, with pictures if possible, and lists of expressions (such as *cracking the egg* in the previous example) will be helpful. Create word walls or posters with academic vocabulary. Provide word banks on handouts. Many teachers create reference bulletin boards with sentence and question prompts so students will be able to express their needs and ask questions.

Beginning students need structure, such as a model of your notes. Later, you might provide sentences with key words or terms left out that the student can fill in during your presentation. Students with intermediate and advanced proficiency will benefit from outlines, graphic organizers, or summarized readings that coordinate with your lessons.

USE RESEARCH-BASED STRATEGIES TO IMPROVE ACHIEVEMENT

Based on research done with colleagues, Marzano (2003) identified nine categories of instruction that serve to effectively increase student achievement. These are particularly valuable to support English learners. Hill and Flynn (2006) applied these principles to English learners (see Table 4.1).

Table 4.1   Selecting Instruction to Improve Student Achievement

Category of Instruction	Implementation	Examples for English Learners
Setting objectives and providing feedback	State intended outcomes of learning in terms students understand and inform students of their achievement.	Set content and language vocabulary objectives to focus student attention; provide timely corrective feedback and help students to monitor their progress; model correct use of vocabulary and grammar.
Nonlinguistic representations	Represent knowledge in pictures or physical sensations, such as movement or using senses.	Have students create "mental pictures" of new words and concepts and draw responses to questions; use pictures, objects, and models to build background knowledge; have students engage in kinesthetic activities.
Cues, questions, and advance organizers	Focus student attention on what is important and significant; use higher-level questions to stimulate critical thinking; activate prior knowledge.	Use a narrative organizer for students to follow; provide visual formats; preview text before reading; use guiding questions.
Cooperative learning	Form heterogeneous groups, in which students learn together with individual accountability and group processing.	Assign small, heterogeneous and homogeneous grouped strategically depending on goals to be achieved with short-term and long-term groups.
Summarizing and note taking	Guide students in identifying and recording main ideas.	Model the steps of keeping, deleting, and substituting information; use visuals; use reciprocal teaching strategies.

Category of Instruction	Implementation	Examples
Homework and practice	Have students practice, review, and apply what they learn.	Individualize homework and practice based on key concepts and skills; make sure students will be able to complete assignments successfully.
Identifying similarities and differences	Have students compare and contrast to process new learning.	Model the process; begin with a topic students are familiar with; use to build vocabulary; use graphic organizers.
Reinforcing effort and providing recognition	Emphasize the effect of one's effort and have students track individual progress in meeting standards; provide praise and rewards as appropriate.	Acknowledge effort and progress, especially with language development.
Generate and test hypotheses	Involve students in inductive and deductive reasoning.	Reduce the language complexity; use vocabulary support, hands-on activities, nonverbal communication, visuals, and manipulatives.

SOURCE: Adapted from Marzano (2003) and Hill & Flynn (2006).

Help Students Process Information

After presenting students with new information, teachers need to pause and give them the opportunity to connect what they have learned to what they know and process new learning. Remember to give students ample wait time to formulate their responses in class discussions.

There are many factors to consider in preparation for a lesson. Box 4.1 offers a summary of the points presented so far for your reference.

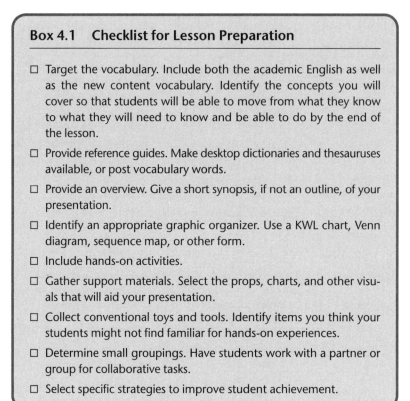

Box 4.1   Checklist for Lesson Preparation

☐ Target the vocabulary. Include both the academic English as well as the new content vocabulary. Identify the concepts you will cover so that students will be able to move from what they know to what they will need to know and be able to do by the end of the lesson.

☐ Provide reference guides. Make desktop dictionaries and thesauruses available, or post vocabulary words.

☐ Provide an overview. Give a short synopsis, if not an outline, of your presentation.

☐ Identify an appropriate graphic organizer. Use a KWL chart, Venn diagram, sequence map, or other form.

☐ Include hands-on activities.

☐ Gather support materials. Select the props, charts, and other visuals that will aid your presentation.

☐ Collect conventional toys and tools. Identify items you think your students might not find familiar for hands-on experiences.

☐ Determine small groupings. Have students work with a partner or group for collaborative tasks.

☐ Select specific strategies to improve student achievement.

During the class session, as you are communicating with students, it is useful to be attentive to several areas of common difficulty. Instead of constantly correcting mistakes, which can be discouraging and humiliating, try to model correct responses. Remind yourself that even though some students may appear passive and withdrawn, they may also be learning in the "silent period." Also keep in mind that they very well might be withdrawn or experiencing some personal difficulties that may require a referral, so learn to recognize the differences. When possible, check for understanding by carefully phrasing questions at students' ability levels, requesting students to illustrate or demonstrate what they know. Finally, identify opportunities for nonverbal as well as verbal response to indicate that the students comprehend the new material or skill.

ADDRESS LEARNING STYLES

Much of our discussion has been centered on generalizations about the way English learners behave, what they need, or what works best. In fact, just as in every other facet of education, there are great individual differences that should be kept in mind. By paying attention to the variety of learning styles evident in the classroom, teachers can better individualize language development instruction. Students will learn more easily and remember more when working in a style that best suits their abilities, personalities, and preferences.

Sensory Modality

The first set of learning styles includes those determined by the senses, with preferences for sight, hearing, or touch. Some students learn best from seeing what is happening. They learn from text material, graphs, charts, pictures, and video. They learn through observation. Teachers who prepare advance organizers and use visual aids will help these students immensely.

Auditory learners favor hearing new information. They are comfortable listening to a story or hearing a presentation. Teachers can help these students by recording information or providing audiotapes, videos, or CDs for review.

Tactile/kinesthetic learners like to move and touch things. Teachers can provide opportunities for manipulating objects, drawing pictures, and acting or role-playing situations. A multi-sensory approach will address all learners.

Global/Analytic Style

This learning style reflects the way people process information. Although most people use both sides of the brain simultaneously, they may have a distinct preference. The global learner uses the right hemisphere of the brain, focusing on spatial and relational processing. This student goes from the whole to parts, looking for patterns and recognizing relationships. The analytic learner uses the left hemisphere for linear processing. This student goes from parts to the whole, looking for details on which to base an understanding. Some students vary their approach depending on the problem, whereas other students use only one way or the other.

Teachers need to model both approaches and provide opportunities for students to practice. For example, a history teacher can present the facts regarding the relative strengths and weaknesses of the North and South prior to the Civil War and ask students to generate conclusions or rank the causes. Later, he or she can present the topic of the Great Depression and have students identify examples.

Field-Independent/Field-Dependent Style

Students vary in the way they solve problems. Timm (1996) reports on the work of Herman Witkin, who explored how a person's perception is influenced by the environment by looking at how people perceive embedded figures from a surrounding field. Students who can differentiate objects from their backgrounds, or who are field-independent, are able to work independently, are intrinsically motivated, and take an analytic approach to solving problems.

Those who are unable to separate items from their surroundings are field-dependent and prefer to work with others, are extrinsically motivated, and take a global approach to solving problems. Students tend to prefer one style over the other. Timm's (1996) research shows that Hmong students tend to be highly field-dependent, whereas other cultural groups lean more toward independence.

Teachers need to become aware of their teaching style. Do you prefer a controlled classroom where students sit in rows quietly doing assignments independently? Or do you structure a variety of paired and small-group activities where students work together on projects? Teachers need to provide activities related to both styles.

Field-independent students like to work alone. They thrive on competition and individual recognition. They work independently of the teacher and try things on their own. Teachers can serve these students by providing them with resources and watching them work unaccompanied. Field-dependent students prefer cooperative learning activities. They like to help others and look to the teacher for explanations and directions. They like concepts that are related to them personally. Many children with limited English fall into the field-dependent style. Teachers can serve these students by working closely with them, having them work together in cooperative groups, and using material that is relevant to the student.

Learners who are field-dependent prefer contextual cues (Jensen, 1995). Field trips, experiments, and hands-on manipulatives support their learning. Field-independent learners do not need the "real thing" and are comfortable in libraries and classrooms looking at videos, books, or computers. The "bicognitive" students are comfortable in both situations.

Impulsive/Reflective

Some students are quick to guess solutions to problems or to answer questions. These students offer impulsive responses. At the other end of the continuum are reflective thinkers. They respond slowly to questions and take their time solving problems. These students do not want to make a mistake and carefully take their time to avoid errors. Teachers must provide ample wait time for these students and provide a supportive climate in the classroom for the reflective thinkers. The other students need to be encouraged to be patient as well. Reflectivity is a behavior practiced in many Far Eastern cultures, for example.

Although research has shown differences in cultural groups related to learning styles, it is dangerous to generalize. Each student should be recognized for his or her unique learning styles and level of proficiency.

Cooperation/Individualism

Another learning style relates to whether a student prefers to work alone or with others. Some students like to work by themselves independently and have their achievements noted. These children may enjoy competition. Teachers who make individual assignments will facilitate the learning environment for these students. Other students would rather work collaboratively with others in small groups. In many cultures, cooperation among children is valued. Teachers who place students in pairs or small groups and structure cooperative learning activities will provide a classroom in which these students will be most comfortable. Of course, students should be given structured opportunities to engage in both grouping situations.

INCORPORATE MULTIPLE INTELLIGENCES

In his research on intelligence, Howard Gardner (1983) originally created several categories: logical/mathematical, interpersonal, spatial/visual, musical/rhythmic, intrapersonal, bodily/kinesthetic, verbal/linguistic, and naturalist. These different styles are also reflected in the ways that people manifest their creativity (Gardner, 1999). The following sections will briefly describe these intelligences and give examples of what teachers can do to help English learners in the classroom.

Logical/Mathematical

Students with logical/mathematical intelligence are able to solve mathematical problems and find numerical patterns. They are able to create reasons for solutions to problems using inductive and deductive thinking. They like order in the classroom and enjoy challenges. They like to categorize information, find sequences, and determine cause-and-effect relationships. They are skillful in predicting and analyzing. Teachers can foster this intelligence by using inquiry methods and project-based learning in the classroom that minimize essay writing and oral speech presentations that require fluency.

Interpersonal

Students with interpersonal intelligence are strong communicators. With their ability to influence others, they will be leaders in the classroom. They work well with others in pairs and on teams. They work toward building consensus in group situations. Teachers can help foster this intelligence by structuring cooperative learning, learning centers, and service learning projects. Many English learners will be more comfortable engaging in informal group settings rather than being in front of the whole class. This will also provide time for the teacher to interact individually with students.

Spatial/Visual

Students with spatial intelligence have a good sense of three-dimensional space. They rely on the sense of sight. They can judge people and items in relation to one another. They are attuned to what is in their environment, and they maneuver easily and find things easily. Teachers can provide rich classrooms for English learners that include artifacts, pictures of objects, and maps. These students like to create art projects and build models that demonstrate what they know. They like to do skits and role plays.

Musical/Rhythmic

Students with musical/rhythmic intelligence can create patterns of sounds. They dance, clap, play instruments, and create music and songs, although singing well is not necessarily a feature. Teachers will find students very sensitive to sounds in the environments. They will find it useful to play different types of music to express ideas and set moods.

Students will enjoy songs, jingles, raps, and chants as methods of retaining information. Assignments can include putting information to music, creating musical performances, or doing projects that include music.

Intrapersonal

Students with intrapersonal intelligence think about how they think; they are highly reflective. They are aware of their own strengths and weaknesses. They need time to reflect and do self-assessments of their progress. They enjoy working by themselves. Teachers can provide private time for students to think and reflect on their interests, concerns, and their solutions to problems. Assignments can include essays, journals, guided imagery, and examining metacognitive skills.

Bodily/Kinesthetic

Students with bodily/kinesthetic intelligence are skilled in body movements and in manipulating objects. English language learners will benefit from using manipulatives and puppets in the classroom. They like to play charades, act out scenes, pantomime, and respond with gestures. They enjoy sports and games. Teachers can have students act out concepts, such as how the parts of a nerve process information or how a bill becomes a law.

Assignments can include options, such as building projects with Legos, Popsicle sticks, or clay.

Verbal/Linguistic

Students with verbal/linguistic intelligence have good language ability and express themselves well. They like to debate and argue in the classroom. They like to read and discuss ideas. Teachers can provide supplementary reading for these students and give them opportunities for discussion in small groups. They also like to teach one another what they know. Teachers can provide opportunities for student research and presentation.

Naturalist

Students with naturalist intelligence understand the natural world. They can recognize and classify flora and fauna. They can discriminate various species. They are interested in animals and their behavior. They enjoy having plants in the environment. They are sensitive to changes in the weather and are fascinated by natural disasters and natural phenomena. Teachers can provide opportunities for students to come into contact with various animals. Science-related activities can include studying the weather and growing plants.

Teaching to Student Strengths

Different cultures emphasize particular kinds of intelligence. Jensen (1995) gives the example of tribes in Africa where all children are taught to sing and play music. Samoan and Fiji islanders are taught to be adept at celestial navigation. Although not all students will excel in every area, providing a variety of experiences in the classroom means that students will all have the opportunity to shine at one time or another. Likewise, students will have the opportunity to improve in their weaker areas. In this way, students of all backgrounds will receive the best we have to give them. Moreover, their cultures, languages, and experiences will be acknowledged and valued (Nieto, 2000, 2002, 2008).

Teachers can design multifaceted lessons that incorporate elements of all the intelligences over the course of a week. In this way, English learners, as well as all the children in the class, will have the opportunity to excel at one time or another. All students will have the opportunity to move out of their comfort range and into other areas. Likewise, assessments can be designed to contain elements of all the intelligences. Jensen (1995) suggests writing the topic or unit in the middle of a piece of paper and drawing spokes outward for each of the multiple intelligences. Then plan the activities and assessments you would use that relate to each area.

In addition, all too often there is an emphasis on mistakes and errors, on what is not working instead of successes. Whenever possible, focus on what students are doing well rather than where they need improvement. Within the field of psychology, for example, one of the newest trends in "positive psychology" is focusing on strengths and resources instead of problems. This means making an extra special effort to help students who are mired in perceived failure to celebrate even minor successes.

USE MULTISENSORY ACTIVITIES TO ENGAGE STUDENTS

Opening lines of communication with English learners can be difficult. Some children may nod their heads or say they understand because they think that behavior is what is expected of them. They imitate what they see the other children do. Some do not want to bring what they see as cultural disrespect on themselves, so they nod and smile. Activities with drama, dance, and drawing can facilitate initial relationships in a nonthreatening environment that can be fun and stimulating at the same time. They also build on the multiple intelligences just mentioned. Using sensory abilities enhances learning and retention (Wolfe, 2001).

Drama

Using drama in the classroom can help English learners with their communication skills in many ways. Students can respond to a prepared script that emphasizes pronunciation or a point of grammar, or they can write their own scripts or just improvise given roles. Acting offers a chance to use vocabulary and grammar and to practice enunciation in a meaningful way. A prop box is a must in the classroom. Acting also calls attention to body language—such as gesture, posture, and social distance—and to the paralinguistic features of language—such as pauses, intonation, and rhythm.

Having children role-play given social situations will be far less socially threatening than having them speak for themselves. It may provide a comfortable way for those students who do not initiate participation to become involved. If a mistake is made, it is the fault of the character, not the student. Students can use a cassette recorder to help them assess their speech. The students can practice by themselves before performing in front of the entire class. The teacher can supervise a rehearsal before the class performance to make sure the students understand the interpretation of the words and to give words of encouragement. Students who do not have roles in the plays will be prepared to follow and participate in discussion about the plays. Drama can be combined with writing and reading exercises.

For the very young or the very shy, try puppet shows or marionettes, in which the speech producer is not even seen!

Song and Dance

Singing can be a great change-of-pace activity. It can be used to energize or relax the students, depending on the selection you make. Just play a cassette tape or CD, and you are ready. Many teachers play classical music as background for their classes, because classical music seems to lower anxiety. Music can be used to calm students and also to energize them (Wolfe, 2001).

Auditory learners like listening activities. Music is highly connected to language: it processes sounds, conveys a message, and strikes an emotional response. Students can also share the music of their cultures.

Using music will contribute to fluency and confidence (Houk, 2005). Singing and rhyming will help with pronunciation as well as with memory. Did you learn the alphabet with the alphabet song? "Head, Shoulders, Knees, and Toes" is a great way to teach parts of the body. Did you learn, "In 1492, Columbus sailed the ocean blue?" Middle school students easily learn how a bill becomes a law by studying the lyrics from *America Rock*, a video by Scholastic Rock, Inc. This strategy is more effective when students create the product themselves (Wolfe, 2001).

Singing will offer the students another means of expression. The lyrics can be used as a topic for discussion. Students can be encouraged to make up their own songs and present them to the class.

Sharing a little of American dance culture—whether through a square dance, a line dance, or the Hokey Pokey—is a great way to get all students up and moving and involved with one another. No language is necessary. Students mimic the leader's actions in time to the music. When they are ready, students can join in the words to the songs. For example, while doing the Hokey Pokey, elementary English learners will find themselves quickly learning the parts of the body. Meanwhile, in a history class, secondary students can be taught the French court dancing of the Renaissance or the Charleston of the Roaring Twenties.

Another suggestion is to have the English learners teach everyone else a few of the dances that are popular in their cultures. Requiring little in the way of verbal explanation, dance is taught primarily by demonstration.

Drawing

Students can record thoughts and feelings and information through drawing pictures or symbols. They can draw their responses to questions or record observations. Students can develop a picture diary of activities carried out in the classroom, like the courtroom artist. All that is needed is paper and a box of crayons—or, for the more technologically sophisticated, a computer. For those who are uncomfortable with drawing, a selection of preprinted pictures or Colorforms might suffice. By asking questions that call for a visual response, you can learn a lot about your students—who the members of their family are, what they like to eat, where they like to go. Their interests, interpretations, and understandings of the world around them will be reflected in their artwork. Drawings can later be labeled as language skills progress. Pictures can enhance vocabulary development. Drawing can be used for small-group projects. Two to four students might be assigned the task of doing a poster or chart related to a topic of study. For example, students of any age and ability could design a travel brochure after completing a geography unit.

You can check students' abilities to follow directions by asking them to perform a set of instructions using pictures. For example, direct the students to put a circle around one item and make a square around another. Or have them move their pencils two blocks east, then two blocks south, to check comprehension of geographic directions. One elementary teacher explains:

> I have them do a lot of drawing. As they become more comfortable with drawing I have them start adding words of English that they have learned and to use them whenever possible. I continue this throughout the year and they are soon to the point of using mostly English.

Drawing can be a useful assessment tool, too. At the elementary level, students can draw the effects of a science experiment, and at the middle school level, students can illustrate stories they have read. At the high school level, students can illustrate a sequence of events.

Another way to use drawing with students is with a Visual/Quote Activity in which students work in groups to respond to and reflect on an assigned reading by creating a poster.

Divide students into cooperative groups of three to five members, and provide a big piece of paper. Give different colored markers to each group member to verify that every student contributes to the poster. Ask group members to discuss the story or reading assignment and select one significant quote and one meaningful visual image from the story. Direct group members to cooperatively create an image and write the quote on the poster. Finally, have groups share their posters with the rest of the class.

This fun and engaging strategy allows English learners to work with a small number of peers. They are able to contribute to the posters in various ways. If their language skills are quite well developed, they may be ready to record the quotes or present the poster orally to the class. If English learners are still at a beginning stage of English proficiency, they may instead choose to contribute to the drawing of the visual image.

The Visual/Quote Activity is a strategy that can be used with expository text as well, with slight modifications. You might have students summarize a key idea rather than choose a significant quote. And students may draw a key concept rather than drawing a visual image, as they did with the narrative text. For example, if students are working on this activity after having read a short textbook passage on photosynthesis, they might choose to draw their interpretation of the process of photosynthesis while explaining key concepts, such as light, carbon dioxide, and water, on their posters.

The strategies in this chapter will help you motivate your students as they learn English and your course content. By structuring your language delivery, scaffolding instruction, addressing learning styles, incorporating multiple intelligences, and using multisensory activities, you will be able to dynamically engage your students in their learning. In Chapter 5 we look, in particular, at building literacy skills.

SUGGESTED ACTIVITIES

1. Interview teachers who work with English learners to find out how they connect with their students and keep their attention. Ask teachers to share their tips for working with this population of students.

2. In small groups, talk to one another about your own dominant intelligence or creativity style and how you have learned best throughout your life.

3. Select a unit of instruction. Identify the new content and academic vocabulary you will need to present. Then decide how you will build background knowledge and what supplementary materials you will need for your students to be successful.

4. Brainstorm a list of ideas for motivating your English learners. Choose from the ideas presented in this chapter. You can also add to your list by discussing this topic in small groups and/or by doing some additional research on the topic of motivating English learners.

5. Record yourself speaking to students. Listen to the recording, carefully considering how clear your speech is. Are you using idioms, acronyms, synonyms, homographs, or noun phrases that might be unclear to your English learners?

CHAPTER FIVE

Building Literacy

The development of literacy skills is of crucial importance for English learners. Today most researchers take a broad view of literacy, suggesting that it involves oral communication skills, as well as reading and writing skills (Scarcella, 2003). Whether we are considering a student's listening, speaking, reading, or writing skills, they each reflect a facet of literacy. To communicate and achieve in academic settings, English learners need to develop proficiency in each of these four areas. The approaches and strategies in this chapter are designed to ensure that your students acquire the literacy skills they will need to be successful in school.

WRITING SKILLS

Writing is often the preferred way for students to show what they have learned; therefore, we explore this area of literacy first. Teachers can choose from among many different kinds of writing activities—such as journals, essays, reports, and letters—as students develop writing fluency. The next sections will provide you with some ideas and strategies for how you might support your students as writers.

The Language Experience Approach

The language experience approach (Nurss & Hough, 1992) is an example of a student-centered technique that ensures the development of relevant materials appropriate for the learners. Students create their own reading material after discussion of a topic in which key words are recorded. They determine the purpose, the form, and the audience for their writing. The teacher or aide writes down the words of the students exactly as they are dictated, and the students copy the text. As students become more capable, they will take on the initial writing, too. Correction is held off until the selection is reread and questions arise. As students reread the selections, they develop their reading ability.

This balanced approach has been found effective with students of all ages. The approach allows students to build on past experiences and incorporate new information with what they already know. Research shows that effective language development takes place when the teacher provides opportunities for students to generate, read, and respond to their own writing.

The writing can then be published or taped for others. Publication of student work not only provides motivation but also validates their work. It provides low-stress support for students learning a new language (Herrell, 2000). This activity can be used in conjunction with any content area and at any grade level.

Journals

The development of writing skills can be promoted by having students complete journal entries. In this interactive process, the teacher responds to the student's entries or asks questions. Initially, students can write words and illustrations. The teacher does not correct the student's writing but may incorporate a correct form of expression in the responses. Prompt feedback is required for this activity to be successful.

There are many benefits to this activity. Students get personal attention from the teacher. The journals provide a way for the students and the teacher to get to know each other. They are both actively engaged in communication. Also, the students can ask questions that they may not be comfortable asking aloud. In addition, journaling on a regular basis helps students to (1) set goals for the future, (2) explore their dreams and future desires, (3) work through personal issues and struggles that they find perplexing, (4) talk to themselves as a way to become reflective, (5) experiment with new ways of thinking and behaving, (6) express and explore feelings that are confusing or passionate, (7) practice writing skills in creative ways, (8) jot down ideas for projects or areas of interest, and (9) dialogue with themselves about any subject they find interesting.

The use of journals is an excellent idea for students at both the elementary and secondary level. At the elementary level, teachers with a single class set of journals might be able to collect and respond to their students' journals on most days. But for secondary teachers, who have many more students each day, the use of journals is often problematic. Most secondary teachers handle this concern by responding to each class set of journals on a different (and constantly changing) day of the week. In this way, they manage to keep up with the journals and still avoid feeling overwhelmed with the constant flood of student journals.

Publishing

Publishing student writing will also help encourage students to work on their writing skills. Beginners will need lots of support. Providing the format, vocabulary word boxes, outlines, and graphic organizers may be appropriate, depending on your students. Students like to have their work read. Publishing their writing in a newsletter or a booklet will motivate your writers. Advanced writers will need help as well. A variety of writing assignments—from book reports to poetry to research papers—will need a full introduction for those who have not been previously exposed to these types of writing assignments. Teachers will need to show examples and explain the requirements of each project.

The key to improving writing is to have students identify real-world purposes for their efforts (Cary, 2000). This means building on student interest, identifying an audience, and emphasizing the process rather than the product alone.

Writing Across the Curriculum

A common approach to teaching writing in many schools today is called "writing across the curriculum." In this approach, all teachers adopt writing as part of their disciplines. By integrating writing into the classroom, learning content is optimized while students' writing skills improve too.

Simply writing more does not necessarily lead to better academic writing. This is especially true for English learners. Teachers need to (1) model effective writing, (2) provide specific feedback on students' strengths and weaknesses as writers, and (3) allow writers multiple opportunities to engage in demanding writing tasks (Scarcella, 2003). By taking an active lead in helping students learn content more effectively, teachers help students develop as academic writers.

When you are looking for the appropriate place to use writing in your classroom, you should first look at those areas of your curriculum that include a language component. In physical education, for example, this might be that part of your class where the rules of the game are learned or a player's responsibilities are detailed. In mathematics, the language component might be found in solving and writing word problems, in writing out the steps required to solve an equation, and finally, in those areas where applications of math concepts to real-world scenarios are taught.

When you focus on the language of your curriculum, it is easy for you to find places to use writing as a tool to help your students learn your course content and develop as writers. As a teacher you are the expert of your content—and of your discipline's unique language. Thus, you are ideally suited to show students how to use the language of their disciplines. This is of crucial importance for English learners, since "English learners will never receive enough exposure to academic English if teachers do not expose them to it in their classes in a rigorous and comprehensive manner" (Scarcella, 2003, p. 166).

This is not to say that fluency-building activities, such as journal writing, quick writes, and learning logs, are not important. They are. It is just important to balance these kinds of fluency-building activities with "accuracy-building activities" (Scarcella, 2003, p. 168), such as essays and reports, since English learners require feedback on the formal features of their writing if they are to grow and develop as academic writers.

POWER

One way to guide English learners through the writing process is to follow a simple acronym. Use the five steps in POWER, which stands for Prewriting, Organizing, Writing, Escaping, and Rewriting, to empower students to be successful writers (Street, 2002).

P—Prewriting

Prewriting strategies allow students the time and structure needed to get their ideas down on paper. It is important to remember that when using prewriting techniques, all student responses should be accepted. This is the place for them to be adventurous and open. Polishing and refining come later. A few simple and common prewriting strategies include

Freewriting. Direct students to simply write nonstop for a determined amount of time. Freewriting offers students a safe way to get words onto the page—free from worries over style, diction, and grammar. Teachers are often amazed at how many ideas will pop into the minds of student writers when they are simply allowed to write freely for a prescribed time period (usually about 10 minutes).

Asking Questions. Take the time for class discussion, and encourage students to ask questions of their instructor and one another to help learners generate writing ideas. They can also list the questions they have that they would like to research or learn more about.

Listing. Ask students to begin listing ideas in the order in which they occur. Also known as brainstorming, this technique allows students to simply list ideas on paper or on a computer. This activity can also be effective as a class exercise, with the teacher recording on the board, a poster, or a computer whatever words students call out.

Talking and Listening. Hold discussions. Conversations, whether students listen, speak, or both, can help generate writing ideas. Students can discuss a topic with a partner, in small groups, or with the whole class.

Wide Reading. Give students time to read silently. Zinsser (2006) suggests that writing is learned by imitation. Reading lays the foundation for writing. One particular way to assist students with idea generation is to provide them with reading material pertinent to the topics about which they will be writing. Wide reading deepens students' reservoirs of experience and language, enabling them to access deeper pools of linguistic resources while writing. Furthermore, wide reading provides rich schema (Rumelhart, 1980) that can be called upon when students begin writing. Books should be provided with reading levels at or just above where English learners are comfortable to move them to the next level of proficiency. Books with pictures and other visual supports, such as graphs and charts, will also be helpful.

O—Organizing

Once students have some ideas, they need to bring a sense of order to the chaos of an initial freewrite or brainstorm. Teachers can assist them with this task during the organizing stage. Oftentimes, English learners have difficulty restricting their subject. For instance, if students are writing papers on homelessness, instructors help writers when they ask students to refine their subject. Rather than homelessness in the United States, students may limit their subject to homelessness in their city. This simple organizing technique of narrowing the subject will help students immensely.

Students may also struggle with the purpose of their writing. By asking students if their purpose is to persuade, to inform, argue, or perhaps to debate, teachers guide students. Determining early on in the process what the purpose will be helps students better focus their writing. Other considerations include clearly identifying one's audience, length, format, and of course, time restraints.

Finally, teachers should not insist that all students adhere to a strict formal outline, for many writers find outlines confining and artificial rather than helpful. Rather, analyze the level of support that students need, and adjust guidance accordingly.

W—Writing

Students need ample time to write. When students are composing drafts of their writing, they are working with the ideas they have on paper; they are really thinking on paper. For this reason, students need opportunities to produce several drafts before submitting a final copy. The more occasions writers have to draft, the more they are able to revise, rethink, and clarify their thoughts.

At this drafting stage, students are writing, not polishing. Perfection in spelling, grammar, and usage should not be expected at this stage. Allowing students to draft in class allows teachers the chance to hold brief conversations and tutorials with students, saving time later when teachers evaluate their students' work (Gallagher, 2006; Street, 2000). Teachers need to emphasize the entire writing process and support students' efforts throughout the process rather than simply marking the final copy.

E—Escaping

Students need to escape from their writing. Writers work better when they can come back and look at their work with fresh eyes (Atwell, 1998; Hairston, 1986; Lindemann, 1995). Thus, escaping from writing may be as important as any other stage in the writing process. Returning to a writing project after a break allows students to see their work with a new perspective and renewed energy.

R—Rewriting

During this phase, students evaluate their thinking. It is an opportunity for students to see that through their writing, their thinking is always evolving. They get a second, or perhaps a third chance to rethink—and rewrite—their initial explorations into a topic. This is also the time for editing for correct spelling, grammar, and usage.

Giving Feedback on Student Writing

Responding to student writing in a timely way is tremendously important. Through comments, teachers let students know what is valued in writing. Therefore, it is important to use a positive tone and coaching approach as well as recognize achievement. Being supportive of students will encourage them to take risks and to continue to revise their work.

Providing students substantial, honest, and accurate feedback *before* the final version is submitted allows students to use feedback to revise their work (Gallagher, 2006; Street, 2000, 2005a, 2005b). The use of scoring guides, rubrics, and student self-assessment guides is especially helpful to students, parents, and teachers, especially when shared before assignments are given (Manzo, Manzo, & Estes, 2001). Even better, collaborate with students to create these tools.

Though English learners will naturally make numerous errors as they develop as writers, teachers should acknowledge those errors as places to begin working with students on the formal features of academic English. You can provide feedback through one-on-one meetings or through written comments on student papers. As you provide English learners with carefully planned writing instruction, they will make significant gains as academic writers.

READING SKILLS

The selection of reading material needs careful consideration. English learners need reading that is just above their level of understanding and that is interesting. Choosing culturally relevant material will make a big difference. If students read about their culture, they will begin to make connections and build upon their prior experiences. Having selections about people who are similar to them validates their experiences. You will need books at all different reading levels to meet your students' changing needs.

Teachers have found that providing many books on one topic enables students to come into contact with the same vocabulary and grammar. What they read in one book will be reinforced in succeeding books. This is called "narrow reading." If you can provide books in the primary language as well, the concepts are sure to be clear to the students. Science and history classrooms, in particular, will benefit from having many resources available to students for research.

Structured Reading Lesson (SRL)

The Structured Reading Lesson is a simple and effective way to develop reading skills. It focuses on instructional activities before, during, and after reading. These three components of the Structured Reading Lesson (SRL) are listed in Box 5.1.

Box 5.1 Structured Reading Lesson Components

Prereading Activities

☐ Draw upon or build background knowledge.

☐ Establish purpose for reading.

☐ Instill curiosity and motivation.

☐ Present vocabulary that may be unfamiliar to students.

During Reading Activities

☐ Focus the students' attention on lesson objectives.

☐ Stimulate discussion centered around the lesson objectives.

☐ Relate prior knowledge to information in the text.

After Reading Activities

☐ Reflect upon the meaning of the text.

☐ Engage students in higher levels of thinking that go beyond surface-level information.

☐ Facilitate oral and written summaries of what was learned.

Prereading Activities

Teachers can do several things to assist English learners with reading. The first is to activate and/or build up students' prior knowledge on a topic prior to reading. The importance of assessing students' prior knowledge on the topic about to be explored in a reading selection cannot be emphasized enough. Simply building up students' background knowledge on the topic to be explored prior to reading will greatly aid reading comprehension. Because reading is more than merely understanding individual words, making connections with prior knowledge is crucial. The second is to set a purpose for reading, and the third is to preview the text.

Ask students to consider what they already know about the subject matter to activate prior knowledge. Find a topic related to the lesson that students will recognize. If students have little or no background knowledge on a topic, spend time to present concepts that are new to students before reading ever begins to construct their background knowledge.

Some teachers like to begin with a simulated experience. For example, when studying industrialization, history teachers have students imitate what it is like to work on an assembly line. Students are divided into groups, and then each group is given a task, for example, measuring, cutting, assembling, and stapling paper for notepads. Economics teachers simulate the marketplace by passing out paper bags filled with odds and ends and allowing students to trade with one another.

Preview the text with your students by reviewing the title, the pictures, charts, and graphs, and the print in order to bring to mind relevant thoughts and memories. Make sure students know all the features of their textbooks. Lead a "treasure hunt" to discover the table of contents, glossary, resource section or appendix, and index. Does the book have a graphic organizer, such as a time line or concept web or list of questions, to guide reading at the front of each chapter? Some textbooks have a list of objectives at the beginning of each chapter to indicate what the student will learn.

Finally, work with students to set a purpose for reading by asking questions related to big ideas about what they want to learn. For other types of reading, the teacher will need to model and discuss the reason directly with students to identify why they are being asked to read a story, a poem, a magazine article, a historical diary entry, a graph, or a newspaper article. For example, they will be reading to gather information, to identify the causes and effects of a particular event, or to identify the author's point of view.

During Reading Activities

Help students become effective readers by having them check their understanding of the text. Ask them questions about the reading. Have students use context clues to figure out unknown words, make inferences, and predict what will happen next. Finally, ask students to integrate new concepts with existing knowledge.

After Reading Activities

To help students become strategic readers, have them summarize what has been read by retelling the important aspects of the reading. Direct students to evaluate the ideas contained in the text and make applications of the ideas in the reading to unique situations, extending the ideas to broader perspectives.

Keeping this basic "before, during, and after" structure for teaching reading to English learners can really make a difference for your students.

Reading Resources

Student dictionaries are a vital classroom resource. A dictionary that is well suited for English learners at the middle and high school level is the *Longman Basic Dictionary of American English*. It has clear, simple definitions and easy-to-understand examples used in typical contexts. Bilingual dictionaries offer an additional resource.

Students should have easy access to libraries. Note that some children will be unfamiliar with libraries and will need not only an introduction but also an orientation to the library collections and how to access them. As some children do not have time to read at home or are not accustomed to reading at home, time in class should be provided. Parents will need to be informed that students are allowed to keep the books for a set period of time and then must return them promptly, as opposed to assigned textbooks, which they keep for the semester or school year. The more students read, the better readers they will become.

Integrated Reading Strategies

KWL

A successful integrated reading strategy is the KWL (Ogle, 1989), in which the teacher begins by identifying what students already *know* (K) about a topic, what they *want* to learn or know more about (W), and then later, when they have finished the unit of study, what they have *learned* (L). This exercise begins by activating students' prior knowledge and serves to identify needed vocabulary for the English learner. You can also incorporate unfamiliar concepts that will be useful in understanding new material. It ends with students summarizing content after they complete the reading assignment.

SQ3R

A second common integrated strategy is SQ3R (Robinson, 1970). Students first *survey* (S) the passage to be read, and then they create *questions* (Q) from headings and words in bold print or read the questions found at the end of the section before they *read* (R) the passage. After reading, they *recite* (R) by creating an oral or written summary of what they have read. Finally, they *review* (R) by answering the questions they created for the passage.

Multipass

Another technique is Multipass (Deschler, 1983), in which students preview information before active reading. To implement this technique, first ask students to read just the headings and subheadings in a passage and develop questions. Then direct students to go through the passage a second time to look at the visuals and read the captions. Next, have students read sentences that have boldfaced words and use the context to determine the meaning of the words. Finally, have students read the introduction and conclusion. Only after students have made these four "passes" through the reading assignment are they directed to do the actual reading.

Think Aloud

With difficult passages, the think-aloud strategy enables you to model and identify the reading strategies you use. As you read aloud, you describe your own thinking process out loud. For example, you show students how you sort through text for the main ideas, try to figure out the meaning of a word from its context, and reread passages that you say are unclear after the first reading. You verbalize the questions you ask yourself as you read, such as "What is this author trying to say?" when you don't understand a passage, or "I think there is going to be conflict" as you predict the ending.

Next you engage students in the think-aloud process and work together to construct meaning. This focuses student attention and forces students to take their time to process what they are reading.

Reciprocal Teaching

Another popular and effective strategy for helping English learners negotiate narrative and informational text is Reciprocal Teaching (Brown & Palincsar, 1984). In this strategy, the teacher and students take turns leading a discussion concerning a text. Though there are many variations, reciprocal teaching involves four comprehension strategies while reading: summarizing, questioning, clarifying, and predicting. It can be used before, during, or after reading to develop students' comprehension skills. This is an especially effective strategy for English learners because students engage in metacognition (thinking about their own reading process) by checking their own understanding of the readings.

With time, students can begin to internalize the kinds of thinking skills implicit in this strategy.

Wide Reading

English learners will also benefit from wide reading (Tomlinson & McTighe, 2006). Allowing students time in class to read texts that they choose is a common practice in many schools. Sustained Silent Reading (SSR) programs are prevalent because students need to be reading if they are to grow as readers. With wide reading comes exposure to grammatical features, new vocabulary words, plot elements, and other facets of reading that tend to be "acquired" when reading (Krashen, 1993).

Processing Information

English learners will need help to process what they have learned. Hill & Flynn (2006) suggest giving students teacher-prepared notes and then teaching them note-taking strategies to assist with comprehension. Teach students several ways to take notes, such as two-column note taking (main idea/detail notes) and webbing. Students can add pictures as they acquire new information, review their notes to reinforce learning, and extend their learning. Taking notes during reading will help focus students' attention on the material.

Depending on the subject, graphic organizers serve as pre-, during-, and postreading activities to help process information. Sequence mapping, character mapping, concept mapping, Venn diagrams, cause-and-effect charts, or problem-solution graphic organizers may be appropriate, as well as completion of the KWL and SQ3R strategies described previously, and note taking. These strategies help students transform the information to make it their own. Students work with new content by summarizing, categorizing, showing relationships, sequencing, and giving additional examples, all of which give them an opportunity to review the material after they have read it.

Addressing Reading Challenges

Reading literature will likely pose a significant challenge for English learners. A story with many subplots may be difficult for them to follow. Poetic imagery may be problematic. Overwhelming detail will be frustrating for them. Drawing inferences can be a challenge. By anticipating these problem areas and addressing them before the actual reading, teachers will structure successful experiences.

Other areas of difficulty to anticipate are the inclusion of unfamiliar names of people and places. Use maps to show locations and time lines to indicate historical periods. Likewise, expect mathematical and scientific terms to be a challenge as well. Show students how to analyze words for prefix, root, and suffix. Practice pronunciation of names and new vocabulary with your students. You may need to break words into syllables as you explain how to pronounce groups of letters.

SPEAKING SKILLS

As we have discussed, students will talk when they are ready. To encourage speech, there are several important points to remember. First, establish a comfortable, safe environment, one in which the students feel accepted and worthy. Second, provide a meaningful situation in which students will be motivated to participate, such as when they serve as the expert in a subject or have had a similar experience to one being discussed. This can be facilitated by taking their interests and individual histories into account.

Pronunciation

With enough exposure, students will repeat what they hear. Younger students will pick up pronunciation on their own (Jesness, 2004). Others may need help. Speech does not have to be perfect, but it needs to be understood. With students who have difficulty, wait until they feel comfortable and are ready to accept help. With these students, you may need to explain and model how to form specific sounds, that is, how to place their lips and tongue. Demonstrate how syllables are accented in words. Pronunciation is a skill they will need to practice. Bilingual dictionaries will be a good resource. Becoming familiar with the students' native languages may help you find points of similarity. Continue to model your speech and encourage students.

Plan for Student Speech

During class, allow opportunities for English learners to speak in their languages of choice, even if their choice isn't English. By providing them with a voice in the classroom, at least with each other, they will feel more comfortable. As mentioned in Chapter 3, it is important to structure questions—from closed questions requiring one-word answers to open-ended questions—so that students will respond according to their level of fluency. English learners need to be taught how to respond to and how to ask questions. Box 5.2 provides a list of suggested prompts to post.

Box 5.2   Ten Conversation Supports for English Learners

Have students select from the following prompts to participate, request clarification, or ask questions.

1. I agree with [name] because . . .

2. I agree with [name], but would like to add . . .

3. I disagree with [name] because . . .

4. If I understand you correctly, you think . . .

5. I hear what you say, but what about . . . ?

6. To summarize . . .

7. I'm confused about . . .

8. Would you please repeat what you said about . . . ?

9. Would you give me an example . . . ?

10. Have you considered . . . ?

Teacher talk needs to be reduced so that student talk will increase (Cary, 2000; Houk, 2005). English learners need lots of time and practice. Students will use what tools they have, beginning with limited vocabulary and gestures, to negotiate meaning in the classroom. Houk (2005) suggests planning routinely to give students opportunities to talk to each other, from time at the beginning of the day to "check in," turning to partner to summarize, ask a question, discuss a point, and/or repeat what was just said.

Students can then share, discuss, and present to each other in pairs, to small groups, or to the whole class, providing for social interaction. Freeman and Freeman (1998) note the following with respect to group work. Students enjoy working in groups; they find it motivating. The amount of language increases, as does the quality of the language. There are all sorts of choices for the teacher, from simulations to structured communication activities to collaborative learning projects.

Holding class meetings (see Chapter 2) sets a tone whereby all students are not only entitled but encouraged to participate. Developing consensus requires students to be able to state their opinions and rationales for their positions on issues. Whether all students agree on a course of action, or a vote is taken by students at the end, all students' speech is valued.

Additionally, one high school English teacher of diverse students, Kelly, builds community by discussing his interests or naming his "territories" (Atwell, 1998). Harvesting the lessons of his life for use in the classroom, this teacher shares his need to write about topics as diverse as his students: Frisbee golf, politics, and coaching high school basketball. He identifies subjects of importance in his personal life, and then he invites his students to examine their own interests and desires. As Kelly's students engage in this process of naming, we are reminded of how important it is for students to feel comfortable and competent if we hope to establish a sense of community in the classroom.

In this way he models how to engage in appropriate classroom discussions. By weaving his interests and those of his students into his writing and speaking activities, this teacher skillfully and purposefully establishes and nourishes a sense of community among his students. As students become aware of other students with similar and different interests, they make connections with others.

Cooperative Groups

In general, cooperative learning involves students working together in small groups in which they are responsible for their own learning as well as that of their teammates. The nature of the task varies according to the particular technique implemented. Using David and Roger Johnson's (1998) learning-together method, students work together to produce a group project. Students following Robert Slavin's (1988) methods are placed in student teams to help each other learn material. Slavin's groups are based on team recognition, individual accountability, and an equal opportunity for success.

Yael and Shlomo Sharan's (1992) group investigation method features a constructivist approach to learning in which students work together to identify problems, plan how to study them, collect information, and present reports in interesting and creative ways. English learners benefit in many ways from cooperative learning activities. As noted previously, cooperative learning groups may be more culturally consistent for some students than whole-class learning. Students receive practice with language as well as practice with content. The teacher can carefully structure the composition of groups to combine students who have strong language and academic skills with those learning English.

The first activities can be designed to build communication patterns and rapport, beginning with nonverbal activities that require each member to participate in order for the task to be successfully completed. This might include putting a puzzle together when each member has a piece, or certain "trust" activities in which children work together as a cohesive team.

If there is more than one English learner in the class, they can be grouped together for support or separated for greater exposure, depending on their needs and your intentions. All students will need to be taught the communication and social skills needed to work in a group and the various roles that group members will take. All students can be taught how to give help and how to explain solutions to problems rather than just supplying answers to questions.

Discussion of the group process should follow the cooperative learning experiences to ensure that group responsibilities (recorder, time captain, encourager, spokesperson, and so on) are divided and that each member has an opportunity to contribute to the group discussion or task. Cooperative groups provide the English learners a nonthreatening situation in which to rehearse responses that will later be called for in front of the entire class. It also will provide them with peer models. Changing group membership after a period of time will increase the number of people with whom students interact.

Cooperative learning has been identified as a strategy to increase student achievement (Marzano, 2003). Cooperative groups provide for repetition of key words and phrases, require content-relevant speech, and reduce student anxiety (Hill & Flynn, 2006). Organize students into small heterogeneous groups, but be careful not to overuse cooperative groups, as students must become individually accountable for their learning and language development. Give students the opportunities to work with others in informal short-term groups as well as formal long-term groups.

Like all the methods suggested in this chapter, cooperative learning groups require you to consider the inner world of your English learners—what it is like for them to be strangers in a strange land. Your job, as much as possible, is to help them to feel welcome. Through the strategies included in this chapter, and many others of your own invention, you are demonstrating how responsive you can be to their needs. As you become more proficient, you will better be able to differentiate your instruction for the students in your classroom.

LISTENING SKILLS

English learners use listening skills all the time. They are constantly searching for meaning (Houk, 2005). They work to make sense of the sounds they hear as they pay attention to the body language, tones, and varying social situations they find themselves in. During a typical school day, English learners are constantly trying to understand the English around them. They are always listening, be it a teacher's math lesson or a friend's story in the cafeteria.

Inside the classroom, speaking and listening skills are typically used more often than are reading and writing skills. Teachers can help their students by teaching active listening skills. Then they can explicitly teach students conversation skills (Bartholomew, 2007; Houk, 2005), such as

- Looking directly at the speaker
- Listening carefully to make sense of the speaker's words

- Using names of speakers to agree or disagree
- Identifying words to use to ask for help ("who," "what," "where," "when," "why," and "how") when they do not understand or need information
- Using words of etiquette, such as "please" and "thank you" and "you're welcome"
- Adding examples or other ideas
- Taking turns speaking
- Summarizing what they have heard

Students must also have a purpose for listening (Pike, Compain, & Mumper, 1997). Preview with students why they will be listening. Are they trying to gain information, to evaluate ideas being expressed, or enjoy an experience, as in listening to a story? Additionally, inform students what they will be expected to do during and/or after listening. Will they write a response, draw a picture, make a chart or graph, or discuss their reactions with another student? The clearer the expectations, the more successful the English learners will be.

Listening exercises, the kind that are used to train counselors and professional helpers, are also useful in teaching anyone more effective communication skills. Basically, this takes the form of pairing students into dyads and then asking one person to speak about something meaningful while the other practices listening—attending fully, using nonverbal prompts (head nods), facing the person fully, and then responding with a brief summary of what was heard. The conversation does not proceed until the talker is convinced that what he or she said was fully understood and captured in the summary statement. This teaches students not only to listen better, but to prove they understood.

Kika: So I was telling you that my sister is a real pain. She always interrupts me, especially when I'm in the middle of something. I can't get anything done—It's so frustrating. I turn my homework in late sometimes because I just can't concentrate with all the stuff going on at home. It's not just my sister, but my parents are always fighting too.

José: You are saying that your sister is a pain. I know just what you mean. I've got four brothers at home, all bigger than me.

In this example, José got the most concrete part of the communication, but missed the deeper content. If a skilled observer was present, José could be helped to try again, but this time, being more detailed:

You are really frustrated and overwhelmed with everything going on at home. Your sister and your parents make things difficult for you. And you sound scared too that you are falling further behind.

Obviously, this second response demonstrates a deeper level of listening, reflecting back not only the content of what was said, but also the underlying feelings.

STRUCTURED COMMUNICATION ACTIVITIES

Instructional approaches that promote integration of speaking, listening, reading, and writing in ways that reflect natural language use are helpful for English learners. But opportunities for speaking and listening require structure and planning if they are to support language development. Teachers can promote effective listening skills by structuring class discussions through partner sharing, group work, and whole-group activities. These kinds of discussion structures have a number of benefits for English learners:

- Promoting reasoning skills
- Enhancing critical thinking skills
- Developing active listening skills
- Refining academic speaking skills
- Creating environments that are rigorous, coherent, and equitable

There are many discussion structures available to teachers. See Table 5.1 for some ideas. You can modify these activities as needed and integrate them with reading, watching a video, and writing exercises before or after the discussions. The teacher or students may generate discussion prompts or questions. Following the activity, have students note relevant comments, locate evidence to support positions, recall active responses made by other participants, and identify examples of drawing another student into the conversation.

Table 5.1   Discussion Activities

Inner-Outer Circle	Students form two rings facing each other. Present a topic or question for students to discuss in pairs. After a limited time, students in one circle move to one side as new partners are formed to revisit the topic or start a new conversation.
Four Corners (Strongly Agree, Agree, Disagree, Strongly Disagree)	Label the corners of your room. Give students a controversial statement and have them move to the label which best reflects their position and discuss their rationales.
	Students discuss their reasoning with their corner group before the class begins discussion on the topic.
Newspaper Bureau	Preview a select group of newspaper articles for students to read. Have students count off (1, 2, 3, 4, 5, 6) and assign sections by number. Rotate each week the section a group reads. Have students read and discuss the assigned section in a small group to become experts. Select a leader from each group to present to the class.
Fishbowl	Have two to four students conduct a conversation in the middle of a circle of students. A leader is selected to lead a discussion. Another set of students stands behind them to serve as advisors in the discussion. The remaining students sit around the circle. Students take turns being in the "fishbowl." Following the conversation, debrief the discussion as a class with respect to the topic as well as the implementation of active listening skills.
Reading From Different Perspectives	Ask students to read a story or article on one topic that involves different perspectives. Then assign students to reread the text focusing on one point of view.
	In small groups or as a class, have students discuss the topic through the assigned perspective as well as compare it to their own thinking and that of their peers.
Role Play	Divide students into small groups. Provide students with descriptions of roles and have them reenact a historical event or solve a problem facing the characters. (Consider adding costumes and props!)

In Chapter 7, we look at ways to incorporate technology to improve listening skills. English learners need time to hear and mimic the language.

RESPONSIVE INSTRUCTION

As teachers get to know their students and the standards they are to address, they plan strategically to meet the needs of the learners. Tomlinson (2003) presents Principles for Fostering Equity and Excellence in Academically Diverse Learners: implement a good curriculum with instruction to stretch the students using flexible grouping, constant assessment, and grading to reflect growth.

It's not always possible to individualize instruction, but teachers can look for "*patterns* of instruction likely to serve multiple needs" (Tomlinson & McTighe, 2006, p. 19). Choose from the strategies presented in this book to help you meet the multiple needs of your students. More ideas follow in Chapter 6 as we look at ideas gleaned from various methods of foreign language instruction.

HAVE FUN

We end this chapter on the topic of play. Learning should be fun. A sense of playfulness will help you succeed in your efforts. It is an effective way to connect with students (Wolk, 2003).

Humor

Through laughter, we feel alive and connected (Kottler, Zehm, & Kottler, 2005). Valuing humor is a way to reach out to students and will help them feel more comfortable. You'll be perceived as a warm and interesting person. Acknowledge when funny things happen in the classroom. They happen all the time.

Games

Students love to play games. There are many games that will reinforce vocabulary, review content, and engage your students. Students will enjoy Twenty Questions, Facts in Five, Pictionary,

Jeopardy, or Tic-Tac-Toe. Students can play in teams as a class or in groups. You can create your own board games or have students create them. Simulate a baseball game on the board where students advance around a diamond or a football game where students move down a field by answering questions correctly. With a Nerf ball, you can have an indoor volleyball game with the right to serve earned by answering questions correctly.

Do the Unexpected

Be dramatic for a change, dress up, or stage a surprise environment for your students to experience when they walk into your room. Novelty will spark student interest. Pose a mystery in your content area for students to solve. Let your imagination be your guide.

SUGGESTED ACTIVITIES

1. Analyze a lesson involving a reading assignment that you have taught previously. After carefully considering what you have learned in this chapter, what changes might you make to this lesson?

2. Consider a lesson where you could include a writing assignment. How will you support your English learners in this writing-intensive lesson?

3. Evaluate the discussion activities listed in this chapter. Choose some to try in your class that would be appropriate for your English learners.

4. Identify a list of books for both wide and narrow reading for your students.

5. Create a list of three or more scaffolds that you could use to support English learners in a reading or writing activity. In small groups, discuss whether or not the scaffolds you chose would be sufficient for your English learners. If not, use the suggestions of your colleagues to expand your list of strategies.

CHAPTER SIX

Using Strategies Borrowed From Language Instruction

Whereas Chapter 5 offered tips on literacy strategies that can be used in a variety of classroom settings, there are also a number of methods that can be borrowed from the work of foreign and English language teachers. These can be adapted in many different ways, depending on your grade level, subject area, teaching style, and particular student needs.

LEARNING FROM FOREIGN LANGUAGE INSTRUCTION

During the course of the past 20 years, the field of education has benefited from a body of research and the work of thoughtful teachers; these have shown that teaching is both a science and an art (Davis, 2006). This balancing act between science and art is an especially apt metaphor when we consider the challenges faced by teachers who need to provide language development for English learners of different ages, varied languages, varying language abilities, and vastly different academic backgrounds (Lachat, 2004).

The work of foreign language teachers offers a variety of techniques that can be applied in the regular classroom to help you work effectively with all your students. Listed here are brief descriptions of some of the more useful approaches, with examples of how to apply them. Some will be appropriate for use with the entire class; others will be more suitable for small groups or individuals. Regardless of which particular programs or techniques you use, research supports the notion that many of the strategies you will use with English learners are simply extensions of approaches that work well with all students (Gray & Fleischman, 2004/2005).

Direct Method

In the 1920s, the direct method of teaching foreign languages became popular in the United States as an alternative to the nineteenth century's reliance on grammar translation techniques to teach classical languages. Speech, with an interest in proper pronunciation rather than writing, was the goal. Teachers of the direct method speak only the language to be learned in class. Lessons are sequenced in progression of complexity. The receptive skills of listening and reading are taught before the productive skills of speaking and writing. Attention is given to the age and background of the student and to relating language to culture.

The direct method emphasizes the fact that age and background have a bearing on language learning ability. It is important to use vocabulary suitable for the age of one's students. As noted in Chapter 1, knowing the backgrounds of your students will help you choose lessons that are motivating and stimulating to them as you teach English through a content area. In teaching the steps of the scientific method, for example, let the students suggest a hypothesis to test, a question they propose, or something they want to know more about.

Today's classroom teachers can benefit from this method by seeing how the use of English is a part of our culture. Even the words are determined, to a great extent, by the cultural constructions of our world. For example, a classroom exercise in a social studies class might ask students to compare (with explanations for English learners) slang words used today versus those used during the 1920s. Ask your students what the modern counterparts are for such terms as *giggle water*, *big cheese*, *bee's knees*, *cat's meow*, and *spiffy*.

The Natural Approach

Communication activities in a low-anxiety setting are central to Krashen's (1996) natural approach, which was developed in collaboration with Tracy Terrell. This method is especially effective for beginning and younger students. The teacher models speech using high-interest, high-context topics to present vocabulary in a controlled manner. For example, the teacher might do an introduction activity at the beginning of the school year by describing the people in the room and asking questions about them.

The teacher guides the students in conversation through four stages. In the first stage, students communicate with nonverbal behaviors—movement and gestures. ("If you have brown eyes, stand up.") In the second stage, students respond to closed questions with one or two words. ("Are your eyes brown or blue?") In the third stage, students speak in phrases or complete sentences. ("I have brown eyes.") In the last stage, students can carry on conversations with minor guidance. ("I know a boy who has beautiful brown eyes and . . .") The teacher gradually adds new vocabulary as the students slowly progress. Students respond at their own pace and are encouraged to realize they don't have to understand every word. The teacher does not correct errors, so anxiety levels are not raised. After the students have developed intermediate oral proficiency skills, reading and writing are added.

An important contribution of this method is the identification of the stages of speech emergence. Teachers can structure their questions according to the ability levels of their students. Those who have very limited proficiency, in the preproduction stage, can be asked to use gestures to indicate a response or circle pictures on a page that represent ideas. Those with low proficiency, in early production stages, should be given yes-no questions or multiple-choice questions in which the answer is supplied. Also effective are sentence-completion exercises or questions that require one- or two-word answers.

When students reach the fourth stage, teachers can ask for information, explanations, and interpretations or give problems for students to solve. As with other strategies mentioned, you do not correct the students' mistakes. The goal is communication.

From the natural approach, the regular classroom teacher once again realizes that students will have to be exposed to a great deal of language before they respond verbally and that they proceed through a series of stages. Activities need to be structured to keep the anxiety level low for students with material that will not overwhelm them.

Total Physical Response

The Total Physical Response (TPR) technique, developed by James Asher (Bowen, Madsen, & Hilferty, 1985), begins by incorporating listening skills with movement. Asher noted that mothers often talk to their children using the imperative, for example, "Turn around," or "Give me the ball." Used primarily with beginners, this approach couples commands with action. The teacher begins by modeling simply stated directions using controlled vocabulary to build language, and students respond with the appropriate action: "Stand!" "Sit!" Then the teacher expands to complete sentences: "Walk to the door." "Open the door." Listening is emphasized, and the students are not pressured to speak. Seely and Romijn (1995) have extended TPR to involve students in more complex dialogues and role-play situations.

In the regular classroom, the teacher will find that new students with beginning English skills will respond well to commands used frequently that relate to classroom routines. Identify the requests you frequently make, such as "Clear your desks," "Take out a pencil," and "Line up at the door." You can call on an individual to demonstrate that the commands are understood. Students are not required to give a verbal response.

Suggestopedia or Suggestology

Georgi Lozanov's (1979) method concentrates on providing a warm, relaxed, pleasant environment. Paying close attention to the students' emotional state, the teacher's approach is to create receptive students. Relaxation techniques and breathing exercises are used to begin each session to enable students to tap their latent ability to learn a language.

Suggestopedia requires an informal setting, such as a living room. Musical interludes are also used for relaxation. The students are given an identity to assume, complete with a distinct personality and profession. The lesson then proceeds over the next several days. First, the teacher introduces lines of dialogue with scripts and gives an informal explanation. Next, the teacher presents the dialogue with three different intonations (normal, soft, strong). Finally, the dialogue is read expressively, set against music. Listening and speaking are emphasized over reading and writing.

Although the format of the Suggestopedia lessons may not be practical, and the informal setting not available in public schools, the regular classroom teacher may find that providing an anxiety-free atmosphere is a good guideline to follow. Creating an attractive and inviting room will set the mood for students of any proficiency for any subject. If there are too many objects or pictures, students may easily be distracted by overstimulation. Color, lighting, and temperature, as well as the size of seats, will affect students' behavior. It is important to make sure the students' physical and emotional needs are being met.

Counseling-Learning or Community Language Learning

Introduced by Charles Curan (1976), the counseling-learning or community language learning approach focuses on the relationships between the people involved. The teacher's role is to understand the needs and feelings of the students learning a language and to help them reach their goal by establishing trust and cooperation in the group. The teacher, who must be bilingual, is known as a *knower* or *counselor-teacher*. At first, the students sit in a circle and are invited to talk to one another in their native language. The teacher is located outside the circle and translates the students' conversations. The students repeat the translations. The statements are taped and played at the end of the lesson as review or as a subject for a grammar lesson.

Students progress through five stages as they gain confidence, increase their ability to speak to and understand one another, and become less dependent on the teacher. As the students become more competent, the teacher becomes more active in asking questions, making corrections, and adding explanations. Finally, the teacher indicates by cue that students are making mistakes or that more appropriate expressions could be used. The students like the control they have over their learning and the group process that fosters cohesion and respect for one another.

The role of the teacher in this approach is that of a consultant. The teacher is no longer viewed as an authority whose task is to criticize. Rather, the teacher's job is to help students feel comfortable and to minimize anxiety. A safe environment is created in which students can explore their feelings, beliefs, and experiences. Attention is placed on group process, and students are encouraged to talk about what is meaningful to them. The teacher guides the students in their discussions. The classroom becomes student-centered. Children's needs for social interaction are acknowledged and met.

In the regular classroom, the teacher will find it helpful to create a seating arrangement that facilitates communication. If possible, arrange the furniture in your room so students can sit in circles to talk to one another. In this way, a student-centered, non-threatening classroom environment is created. When students sit in rows or at opposite ends of tables, it is difficult for them to interact with one another. Then find connections to the students' lives so the class discussion is meaningful and relevant.

A Note on Group Processes

In our mobile society, many children are often faced with moving to a new neighborhood, learning their way around a new city, meeting new people, and making new friends. Teachers can help students recognize the wide range of feelings associated with adapting to new situations, help students develop support for one another, and help them develop the social skills they will need to be successful in dealing with these changes—which often can be traumatic. Similarly, other personal or community issues can be addressed through group activities.

Small groups or a fishbowl structure (in which a small number of students are selected to sit in the middle of the room while the remaining students observe) can facilitate discussion of such topics as moving, peer pressure, family relationships, school traditions, or community issues.

In order to introduce this structure, a small group of volunteers (8 to 10 is ideal) is invited to form a circle in the middle of the room. Those who are left are asked to form a circle surrounding the inner circle. These students are given a specific assignment and responsibility, that is, to pay attention to the dynamics and processes in the inner group. Students can be instructed about what to look for: Who speaks for you in the group? In other words, among those who share in the group, with whom do you most identify, or whose statements are most similar to the way that you feel?

Those in the inner circle are encouraged to talk about some theme that is important in their lives. They may be instructed to use only "feeling statements," such as "I feel scared to be in the middle like this with everyone looking at me. I'm afraid I might say something stupid and everyone will laugh at me."

Your job, as group leader, is to make sure that all students have a chance to express themselves, even those with limited English skills. The most challenging part is to make sure that everyone in the group (and outside) is patient, respectful, and responsive, so that everyone feels heard.

After a 20-minute discussion, those on the outside of the group can be asked to talk about what was sparked for them during the fishbowl. That way, everyone in the class becomes actively involved. The key to making this work is to make sure that even the quiet students have a forum to speak, and that the few highly verbal members of the class don't dominate things. One way to structure this is to allow students to speak only one time. Another is to use a one-minute timer.

Notational-Functional Approach

One of the most recent approaches to language learning, the notational-functional approach, first identifies the communication needs of students and then structures lessons around those needs. The social situations (home, work, leisure activities, transportation, health facilities, and the like) and social roles are identified. Then the concepts (time, money, and so on) related to those settings are ordered for presentation. Vocabulary and grammar are then integrated as the student learns the functions of language—for example, how to make a statement, ask a question, make a comparison, or express feelings.

The notational-functional approach helps the regular classroom teacher become aware of the language skills students need for their daily lives. Language related to school and the community will be of primary importance. The teacher will need to assess which skills students possess and which they need to acquire (see Box 6.1).

Box 6.1   Daily Living Skills Requiring Communication

Determine if students can perform the following tasks:

☐ Introduce themselves

☐ Follow street directions

☐ Fill out forms

☐ Ask for help

☐ Read and order from a menu

☐ Read and follow directions on medicine labels

☐ Pay for items with our currency

☐ Pass the driver's license test

☐ Understand commonly used idioms

☐ Obtain social services

With English learners, the classroom teacher may have to determine what language skills are most necessary for survival. A good way to begin is to focus on the roles of the students— student, family member, baby-sitter, dishwasher, athletic team player, and so on. Intermediate and advanced students can be asked what they need to know and to bring in examples. Role plays and simulations would be the corresponding models of teaching to implement. These tasks correlate well with social studies units in elementary school, but they will need extra attention at the secondary level.

Special consideration can be given to signs in the community, information in newspapers, ads on television and radio, and bulletins from government agencies. Older students may need help with papers related to employment contracts and job benefits. Other topics might include leases, rental fees, and insurance.

APPLYING STRATEGIES USED BY ENGLISH LANGUAGE TEACHERS

Besides approaches to foreign language learning, we can use models that have been developed by English language teachers as a separate discipline. We will examine how regular classroom teachers can adapt strategies from the Cognitive Academic Language Learning Approach (CALLA) and then Principles for Success. Finally, we look at the Joyful Fluency Model, which incorporates principles from brain research into the development of language.

Cognitive Academic Language Learning Approach (CALLA)

Chamot and O'Malley (1989) developed a program especially designed for the intermediate English language learner. CALLA is targeted for students who have developed social communication skills but are not ready for grade-level academic work. For example, these students need help transferring concepts from their native language to English. In the CALLA classroom, the teacher identifies and presents not only academic language skills but also specific academic content and corresponding learning strategies. Chamot and O'Malley group the learning strategies into three categories: metacognitive strategies, which monitor comprehension; cognitive strategies, in which students interact with the content material; and social-affective strategies, in which students interact with others to help them learn material and demonstrate a positive attitude. Students practice until they become proficient. With this background, students are carefully prepared to enter mainstream classes.

There are five phases in the CALLA lesson. In each phase, the teacher identifies the specific content and appropriate learning strategies. The teacher prepares the students by introducing new vocabulary and then activating learning strategies, such as elaboration (evoking prior knowledge, providing advance organizers), previewing what is to come, and selective attention (pointing out key vocabulary and concepts). During the presentation of material, the teacher presents the new information or skill by direct instruction with additional learning strategies, such as elaboration, note taking (see Box 6.2), checking for comprehension, inferring, and imagery. The third phase involves structured practice.

Preferably, the students will be involved in an application of a hands-on activity, either individually or in groups. Students apply learning strategies, such as planning for a task, using resources, summarizing information, creating a graphic organizer, or asking questions for clarification. The fourth phase is the evaluation stage, in which both students and the teacher assess what was learned in terms of the identified objectives. The last phase is for expansion, where students will continue to use what they have learned or apply what they have learned to a new situation. Students also develop test-taking skills by reviewing the format of tests, such as the process of "bubbling" responses on a Scantron form and strategies for selecting answers to multiple-choice questions.

Box 6.2   Taking Notes in a "T" Format

Structure note taking to help English learners develop sound habits for listening to, retaining, and organizing new material:

☐ Main ideas are written on one side of a paper and supporting details on the other side.

☐ Students practice speaking by reviewing the notes they have made, usually with a partner to minimize performance anxiety.

☐ During the sharing, each student takes notes on what the other student is talking about, listing additional main ideas and supporting details.

Principles for Success

Freeman and Freeman (1998) developed a set of guidelines for teachers who work with students who do not speak English well. Their principles for success include the following:

1. Design Curriculum Around Themes

Based on the concept that learning proceeds from whole to part, students need to see the whole picture, the big idea, before concentrating on the details. For example, when learning to speak, children use phrases to represent whole ideas, such as *more* for "I would like some more" or *cookie* for "I want a cookie." With early spelling, children use letters, often consonants, to represent words, leaving out vowels or silent letters. With respect to reading, the idea of whole-to-part is supported by setting the purpose for reading, as presented previously.

Thematic units enable English learners to see the whole picture and make connections to their own lives and experiences. Then they can explore details and find specific examples. Change, cooperation, conflict, and movement—these are concepts that all students can relate to. The vocabulary will be reinforced as it is used in multiple situations and can be adjusted according to the ability of the students.

2. Create Learner-Centered Activities That Build on Students' Interests and Actively Involve Them in the Learning Process

Establishing writing workshops is a way to foster a student-centered classroom. Using books, journals, and Web sites, students can explore the answers to what Wiggins and McTighe (2005) refer to as "essential questions" and publish their results. Think of the essential questions as umbrellas under which smaller, more precise questions fit. Build units of study around these smaller questions, or divide the unit of study and have small groups research and present sections to the whole class. The objective is to excite students about finding the answers to the questions so that they will be motivated and engaged in learning activities.

Some teachers establish learning centers or stations, usually located at the side of the room, where students work individually or in small groups at specific times or when they finish an assignment early. Supplementary materials and resources for projects can be provided. Students may even be given the opportunity to use a computer for research, for presentations, and/or to access the Internet.

3. Select Lessons That Will Have Meaning for the Students and Engage Them Directly

The purpose of each lesson must be clear to students for them to use their energy to get involved. The regular classroom teacher can use authentic reading and writing activities and choose relevant themes and topics.

4. Involve Students in Social Interaction

Students negotiate meaning with one another and therefore need opportunities to work together in pairs and small groups. The regular classroom teacher can structure small-group cooperative learning tasks. English learners will have the opportunity to express their ideas, check their understanding, ask questions for clarification, and improve their conversation skills. Active student participation increases when students work in groups. The classroom teacher then has time to circulate and give individual attention to the students.

To be successful, the following factors need to be addressed: organization of resources, clear directions, announced time limits, and time to report back to the class. Social studies teachers can use simulation activities to provide social interaction embedded in the mastery of content. Interact, a company that produces classroom simulation activities, has a range of topics at different levels related to U.S. history and world history. Teachers' Curriculum Institute's History Alive! Program for U.S. and world history also offers excellent materials. English or language arts teachers can use pen pal letters and literature circles as the purpose for social interaction. Cross-age tutoring is another program consideration when working with students from different grade levels. Service Learning and active citizenship projects are other ways for teachers to get students involved in their community, identify problems, research solutions, and select the best one for implementation. We the People: Project Citizen has student guides available in English and Spanish.

5. Develop Lessons That Develop Oral and Written Language Skills Simultaneously

English learners need to be introduced to reading and writing from the beginning. Even beginning students need exposure to both speech and print. Naming and labeling are the first steps. Art, music, and drama activities will help students develop a foundation on which communication skills can grow.

6. Recognize the Students' First Languages and Cultures

Current research (Krashen, 2005; Thomas & Collier, 1997) shows that bilingual education is often the most effective delivery system. Often students who have been in a bilingual setting do better academically, possess higher self-confidence, and show a more positive attitude toward school. Students learn concepts best in their first language and are able to stay on track to graduation. They learn the academic content and critical thinking skills needed to be successful. In the best of circumstances, they transfer these skills to English as they gain more experience and practice. As noted earlier, when students feel that their culture is valued and that they have contributions to make, they feel better about themselves and their roles as students in school.

7. Show Full Faith in the Potential of the Learner

Maintaining a positive attitude and appreciating the contributions of each child will show your support. Many English learners will identify the one teacher who made a difference in their lives by taking the time to show interest and encourage them. Express confidence in their ability. Acknowledge their progress. Be positive and enthusiastic.

BRAIN-COMPATIBLE SECOND-LANGUAGE ACQUISITION

As Dhority and Jensen (1998) explain, creating a joyful environment will facilitate language learning. The teacher's goal is thus to facilitate an atmosphere in class that makes learning fun and exciting. Their Joyful Fluency Model incorporates the following brain-compatible principles:

1. Language learning involves the whole brain. Both hemispheres are active in the process.

2. The brain looks for meaning. Learning lists of vocabulary makes little sense. Using words in a relevant context that has personal meaning for students does make sense.

3. The brain works best in settings that are moderately challenging and that provide high levels of feedback. Although students need a lot of feedback on their speech, it does not need to come solely from the teacher. Peer interaction is desirable.

4. High stress or threat creates anxiety, which is counter-productive. Low stress is preferable, in that it causes individuals to be attentive. Arrange the furniture in your room so it will be comfortable. Set realistic expectations and deadlines. Stay away from sarcasm and anything that would embarrass students.

5. The brain thrives on processing a constant stream of audio, visual, and tactile information. Students need a stimulating environment.

6. Much of what we learn is acquired rather than "studied." Students need multisensory experiences in which student involvement and interaction with others are key elements.

7. Emotions influence student learning. Whereas negative emotions can turn students off, positive emotions will spur students on. Be aware of students' emotional states.

8. The brain creates learning pathways, rather than "memories." All learning can be retrieved if the right pathways are stimulated. Short, student-meaningful, event-oriented situations are compatible with the way the brain learns. Kinesthetic, multisensory experiences are most conducive to this goal. The brain needs time to process new information. Short periods of reflection are key to retention.

9. Learning is a total-body experience. The brain is sensitive to light, smell, touch, sound, and movement. It is easier to remember experiences that involve different parts of the body. The physiological state of the body affects how the individual learns.

10. The brain has developed to specialize in communication. We are social beings. Students should be given multiple opportunities to talk to one another in role plays, debates, discussions, brainstorming sessions, and cooperative group activities.

11. The brain uses language as a form of communication instinctively. Although teachers can aid in the process, students acquire language from exposure to it, rather than direct instruction.

The Joyful Fluency Model emphasizes the role of the teacher as a facilitator rather than an instructor. He or she is responsible for creating a positive, caring atmosphere in the classroom; fostering constructive attitudes; showing concern and appreciation for each student; and encouraging students to work together.

The teacher structures the learning for all students who work individually and in groups in a multisensory environment that is pleasant and comfortable for students. Physical factors to consider are lighting, temperature, furniture arrangement, background music, and peripheral stimuli. Natural lighting, living plants, ventilated rooms, and chairs and tables that can be easily rearranged are recommended. There should be ready access to easels, flip charts, or white boards, with visual aids posted on bulletin boards.

The final consideration is that of selecting materials that will be appropriate for students—not too easy, not too hard. Look for handouts and graphic organizers that are easy to read and colorful if possible. Organize supplementary materials and supplies so that they are readily accessible. Computers are a powerful technology for English learners. Use multimedia presentations, demonstration, and simulations. In Chapter 7, we look at how to use computers and other technology in the classroom.

A Review of Concepts

Based on the methods previously described, the following review chart will serve as a reference for creating a positive social environment and support planning lessons for your English learners.

SUMMARY OF STRATEGIES ADAPTED FROM TEACHING SECOND LANGUAGES

1. Teach English through content.

2. Choose suitable vocabulary.

3. Identify words as part of culture.

4. Use high-interest, high-context topics.

5. Expose English learners to basic vocabulary.

6. Recognize stages of speech production.

7. Select questions according to ability.

8. Use physical responses.

9. Identify requests that are commonly made.

10. Check for comprehension through the use of gestures, actions, and references to pictures or words on paper.

11. Provide a warm, relaxed environment.

12. Use relaxation techniques.

13. Incorporate music.

14. Read with different expressions.

15. Arrange seating in a circle for student conversation.

16. Acknowledge psychological and social needs.

17. Build trust and cooperation.

18. Use group activities as much as possible.

19. Let students talk about what is important to them.

20. Assess and teach language skills needed for daily living.

21. Identify students' social roles and social situations.

22. Use role-playing and simulation exercises.

23. Have students practice learning strategies and apply them to a new task.

24. Organize objectives into short, meaningful, situation-oriented events.

25. Include periods for reflection.

SUGGESTED ACTIVITIES

1. Discuss with a colleague how to structure a low-anxiety atmosphere in the classroom. Consider arrangement and type of furniture, lighting, temperature, sound, and displays.

2. Design a seating pattern in your classroom to facilitate communication among students.

3. Create a series of learning centers which feature supplementary materials, supplies, and resources for small group projects.

4. Observe a teacher who has successful experience working with English learners. Discuss strategies demonstrated and the rationale behind them.

5. Integrate partner and small-group activities in your instruction so students will not only engage in cooperative learning tasks but also improve communication skills.

CHAPTER SEVEN

Integrating Technology

S o much of a child's introduction to the English language comes not through formal schooling but through various media, such as television, radio, popular music, computer games, and the Internet. Many of these technologies can be used to support and strengthen work that takes place in the classroom. Through the use of technology, you can enhance independent student inquiry while supporting the development of students' literacy, language, and critical thinking skills (Wilhelm, 2004; Schrock, 2002; Street, 2005c).

A variety of equipment is available to classroom teachers to support English learners. Cassette, digital and video recorders, televisions, telephones, SMART Boards, and computers can all be utilized to help individualize and personalize your instruction. Ultimately, as a teacher it is crucial that you serve as both a facilitator and coach (Cassutto, 2000; Muir-Herzog, 2004) by guiding students through lessons that use technology (Street, 2005c). Your students will benefit if you do a trial run with any technology-based lessons before you try them with students. This way, you will have experienced what you are asking your students to do prior to expecting them to work on their own or in small groups.

TELEVISION

Children in many parts of the world have been known to surprise their parents by having learned English entirely from watching television, using the World Wide Web, and listening to popular music. "Our parents used to talk in English," an Icelander reports, "whenever they didn't want us kids to understand what they were talking about. But what they didn't realize is that we had picked up so much English just from watching comedy shows on television."

Among all of the instructional devices, this Icelander found old reruns of *I Love Lucy* to be the absolute best English teaching tool. "Lucy's face was so expressive and she used her whole body when she spoke, flailing her arms and contorting her face, that I could usually figure out what she was saying just from her gestures." The Icelander became thoughtful for a moment before continuing his story. Then he broke out into an uproarious laugh. "I just remembered something," he said with a giggle. After a bit of prompting, he continued. "Well, the one thing I could never figure out is why Lucy called her best friend 'asshole.' That just seemed so rude, especially for American TV which is so restricted."

"What are you talking about?" we prompted him, utterly confused by what he was talking about. Lucille Ball would never have used a swear word like that, especially in the 1950s.

"Well," he explained, snickering, "it took me the longest time to figure out that Lucy's best friend wasn't really 'Asshole,' but 'Ethel.' They sure sounded the same to me."

Indeed, just imagine all the mistakes in understanding that people make when they are learning English from the media. Nevertheless, watching soap operas, music videos, cartoons, children's programming, and situation comedies are among the best ways for students to sensitize themselves to English sounds and usage.

TELEPHONE

In checking for comprehension and developing social skills, consider exercises using the telephone. Students can call for information from prerecorded messages. For example, information about businesses and their services can be obtained by telephone. For a broader project, integrate language arts, math, and social studies to have students plan a trip and obtain airplane arrival and departure times, weather information, hotel prices, and museum hours of operation.

AUDIO RECORDING

There are many ways to use audio recorders in the classroom. To begin with, you can record a presentation for students to play prior to a class lesson—or it can be replayed at a later time. Students then have the opportunity to digest small pieces of information at a time. It is a good way to have students focus on pronunciation. For example, after hearing new words or phrases, they can say them aloud and then compare their expression, pronunciation, and phrasing with yours: "I pledge allegiance . . . to the flag . . . of the United States . . . of America."

You can record questions for those students who can't read or have trouble reading. In turn, they can answer on paper or record their responses and give them to you. They will have a chance to practice their answers. They can hear each answer and be sure it represents what they want to say. In this way, they do a self-evaluation.

You can prerecord material, special directions, or comments to go along with a textbook or other printed matter for those learning to read. Of course, there are many book sets of stories that come with audio components already available. By exchanging recordings, you can build a special relationship with your students. Not only will you get to know them better, but this practice will also provide another vehicle for them to practice their language skills in a private way. Working with an audio recorder will allow you to differentiate your lessons. You can prepare material for preview, review, practice, or enrichment.

VIDEO RECORDING

Many school districts have sophisticated equipment available for classroom use. By videotaping a presentation for later playback, you will enable the students to see instruction, demonstrations, and examples that were part of the instruction. Again, students can follow the lesson at their own pace.

Students can make videos to carry out assignments and develop creative projects. For example, they can research the amount of graffiti in the streets, or the number of people using public transportation can be shown on a screen, allowing the English learners to be involved in activities and carry out research that requires technical skills rather than reading skills.

Video can also be used to record progress. Periodic taping of students' involvement in activities will allow the students to see how their language skills are progressing. By viewing the video with supervision, students can also become aware of their body language and evaluate its appropriateness.

Of course, DVDs are a great resource to provide background knowledge for a new lesson and illustrate new concepts being introduced.

COMPUTER TECHNOLOGY

Most children will have the opportunity to use computers in the classroom. Computers not only stimulate motivation but also offer a variety of activities. Computer technology is useful as a way to deliver instruction, as a means for practice, and as a tool for assessment. Students can work individually, in pairs, or even in small groups. They can use computers to work at their own pace on self-directed projects. Students take great pride in the work they produce. They can develop slide presentations and podcasts. With the support of printers, students can publish brochures, books, stories, and reports. They can also produce banners, cards, and posters.

Supportive and Instructional Software to Introduce English

For those just beginning to learn English, drawing programs, such as Kid Pix, allow students to combine graphics with labeling, building up vocabulary and spelling. Or students can scan their own drawings into the computer and import them into whatever software they are using. The illustrated words and terms can then be used as the basis for sentences and later, when students are more advanced, for writing stories and reports. Other suggestions for using pictures as stimuli to encourage students to respond are presented in Chapter 4, in the section on drawing.

For young students, there are software programs now available to introduce letters and words. Such programs will be helpful with students beginning to read. There are games, puzzles, and drills as well as stories to provide practice. There are drill and practice programs at basic levels to support reading development. They help to increase fluency of reading skills. The popular Reader Rabbit program can diagnose students' reading ability and promote letter recognition and rhyming words (Ryan & Cooper, 2007). Available in game formats, these types of programs provide immediate feedback to the user and plenty of practice.

Reksten (2000) suggests using computer programs to reinforce math skills as students represent numbers with objects. For older children, there are many educational games, such as the ever-popular *SimCity, The Oregon Trail,* and *Decisions, Decisions!*

Typing tutorials help students develop the keyboard skills they need. There are writing programs to help students through the composing process. Students can create plays, surveys, interviews, poetry, letters to pen pals, as well as essays. For more advanced students, desktop publishing programs will enhance newspaper production with the use of structured formats and insertion of graphics.

As early as kindergarten, students can learn to select and use software programs to type numbers, letters, words, and sentences and to draw pictures to illustrate their ideas (Reksten, 2000). Even at the first-grade level, students can use multimedia software, such as PowerPoint or HyperStudio, to demonstrate sequencing of a story. Pictures, text, or both can be ordered chronologically by the students in sequential frames. Children can also create their own stories in this way.

Word Processing

Students should continue developing their computer skills with word processing and graphics. As writing increases, students can use editing features for spell-checking, grammar correction, and formatting. Also, production software, such as Classroom Publisher, allows students to produce newsletters and brochures. As keyboarding skills improve, students will be able to type more quickly and accurately.

The word processing capabilities of computers allow students to concentrate on what they are trying to say without being bogged down by the slowness of handwriting, erasing, and correcting or by looking words up in the dictionary. The features of spell-checking, thesaurus, and grammar-checking alleviate the worry out of the technical aspects of writing. These tools allow students to receive the support they need in order to express ideas.

One teacher realized the power of word processing software with English learners when teaching writing in a computer lab:

> For many of my students, word processing software was new. They were amazed at how the process of revision was aided by the software. Gone was the drudgery of rewriting the entire paper to correct errors. Now they were able to compose, edit, and revise their work using simple keystrokes. With the ability to write and rewrite on the computers, the students' attitude toward writing improved, as did their fluency!

Desktop publishing software, such as Adobe InDesign, offers a unique opportunity for students to build their own electronic dictionaries and encyclopedias with graphics. Other projects might include creative writing magazines, school handbooks, instruction manuals, yearbooks, catalogs, and calendars. The possibilities are endless. These activities give students opportunities to develop and practice not only reading and writing skills but also the social skills needed for collaboration.

Word processing can also be used to help students learn to read using the language experience approach described in Chapter 6. As their words are keyed into the computer by others, students come into contact with meaningful print. They will be encouraged to continue writing, or, in this case, typing on the keyboard, in a purposeful manner to increase their reading skills.

E-Mail

With e-mail capability, your students can communicate with others all over the world. They will have an audience for their writing. Whether to exchange letters, to seek information, or to collect information for a research project, e-mail can open the doors of your classroom by promoting active inquiry.

The whole concept of pen pals has been made so routine that students can easily communicate with dozens of friends in every part of the world. Some teachers have combined such vehicles with videoconferencing between classrooms so that students can actually see the people with whom they are communicating. This structure works especially well when students from foreign countries are able to arrange partnerships with their former schools.

Telementoring

Today, a teacher no longer needs to serve as the sole expert in the classroom. It is possible, for example, for teachers and students to learn about plate tectonics from geologists studying earthquakes, or to discuss human anatomy with medical students involved in cadaver dissections. Volunteer subject matter experts (SMEs), such as the geologists and medical students mentioned previously, can work remotely with students, developing mentoring relationships and assuming a portion of the responsibility for the learning process that occurs during their interactions with the students. This practice—known as "telementoring" (Harris, 1998)—is only possible due to changing technologies, such as e-mail and live chat.

Telementoring relationships can provide English learners with authentic situations in which they are asked to communicate with professionals outside of a school setting. At times, students may communicate in their first language to gain information or answers to questions, enabling them to then serve as a resource to the other students in the classroom. To learn more about connecting with volunteer SMEs through e-mail, or to learn more about telementoring, this site provides a wealth of online resources and support: http://emissary.wm.edu/.

Reading Support

Reader software, such as Arkenstone's WYNN (What You Need Now) reader or CAST's eReader, allows text material to be scanned into a computer. Then students can follow the print as it is read aloud. A middle school teacher explains:

> While it takes a considerable amount of time to begin using reading software, once the task is complete, it can be used over and over again. I found that graphs and charts and pictures did not scan well, so I just used text for my students. This made a great difference for my ELL students.

It is easy for the teacher to include special directions, point out new words that students will encounter, and preview the section before the students begin the actual reading. You can link the new material to what has been previously studied and emphasize the important ideas or significant events. This program also allows students to change the presentation. They can edit, highlight, and take notes.

Readability Statistics

Another useful reading tool is the readability statistics feature, available in Microsoft Word, and in other word processing programs as well. This feature allows you to quickly get a readability score for any piece of writing that you can open with Microsoft Word. It can be used when students are asked to read an article on the Internet. You can simply cut and paste the text from the Web site into Microsoft Word and run the readability test. Then you will be able to decide if the text is too difficult for your English learners to comprehend.

The Flesh-Kincaid Grade Level score, a formula based on the average sentence length (ASL) and average number of syllables per word (ASW), lets you know if the reading level of the document is at the grade level appropriate for your students. Additionally, two other measures are provided: Passive Sentences, where a lower percentage is better than a higher percentage, and the Flesh Reading Ease score, determined by a different formula using ASL and ASW, based on a 100-point scale, where a higher score—60 to 70—is preferred.

This feature is also helpful when writing letters to parents and crafting class newsletters for others to read. You might also use it after scanning a passage from your textbook or other print document and pasting it into Word to determine if you need to adapt the text (rewrite portions or add comments, definitions, captions for pictures, and so on) for your English learners.

To turn on this feature in Microsoft Word, simply follow these steps: Tools → Options → Select Spelling & Grammar and check the box for Show Readability Statistics. Then, each time you run a spelling and grammar check, you will also get a readability score for the document. This will be very helpful as you make sure that your students are being exposed to readings that are appropriate for their reading level.

Writing Support

The Web has emerged as a fantastic resource for writers of all ages and skill levels. Dictionaries, thesauruses, and encyclopedias are available digitally. Teachers and students will benefit from online resources supporting development of sentence formation, paragraph construction, grammar, mechanics, essays, and various writing styles, not to mention facts. Box 7.1 has a list of sample resources for students and teachers.

Box 7.1   Sample Online Resources for Students

American Heritage® Dictionary of the English Language
http://education.yahoo.com/reference/dictionary

CIA World Factbook
http://education.yahoo.com/reference/factbook/;_ylt=Atclv_x.zz16fJ
xoa0EqP.JUt8wF

Columbia Encyclopedia
http://education.yahoo.com/reference/encyclopedia/;_ylt=AqmbyK
zwjNZ9NI2ElUw2fyMoCcsF

OWL (Online Writing Lab) at Purdue University
http://owl.english.purdue.edu/handouts/esl/

Roget's II: The New Thesaurus
http://education.yahoo.com/reference/thesaurus/

UCI Correction Symbols at University of California, Irvine
http://e3.uci.edu/programs/esl/symbols.html

Databases

For all students, creating databases will give them the chance to collect and analyze information as part of a science, mathematics, or social studies project. Students can generate hypotheses, collect and record information, and evaluate the results as they explore the world they live in. Data can be gathered by observation, survey, or interview. The type and amount of information collected will need to be carefully structured so as not to be overwhelming or unmanageable. Older and more proficient students can move beyond categorization to develop their own research questions and determine how they will collect the information they need. English learners can easily manipulate data with minimal language. Databases also store information that students can retrieve as they study a particular subject for an oral or written report.

Using spreadsheets is a popular way to handle information. These can be used in mathematics lessons, because they allow mathematical operations to be performed through the application of formulas. Lessons can then be combined with graphing exercises. Students can observe changes taking place in real or simulated exercises.

Handheld Computers

Palm and other handheld computers give students the opportunity to easily manipulate information in a variety of locations (Patterson, 2000). Software, such as ImagiMath, used with handheld computers, helps students to see graphing solutions and then print them. Science probe attachments, such as ImagiProbe, enable students to go into the field and take measurements that can be analyzed at a later date. Students enter data from observations and then upload information to a computer to create databases. Software programs also allow students to store vast quantities of information. English learners can easily participate in these activities.

Podcasting

A podcast is a digital file (audio and/or video) that you download from the Internet. After you download the file, you can listen to it on a computer or on an MP3/portable music player (for example, an iPod). Though audio is the most popular format, video podcasts are gaining popularity. As well as listening to sounds, students can watch corresponding still images, animations, and video.

One obvious advantage of a podcast is that once it has been downloaded to a computer or transferred to an MP3 player, it can be replayed anywhere at anytime. A simple way to think of podcasting is as a form of digital radio that can be played anytime. Podcasts can be used in face-to-face settings; or, they may be used to connect with learners at a distance. They are particularly helpful when students miss class due to illness or other reasons.

One high school teacher uses podcasting to leave lesson plans for his substitute teachers:

> The afternoon before I am going to be absent from school, I create a podcast with instructions for the substitute teacher. Then when the substitute arrives in the morning, he or she simply accesses the podcast to listen to the day's plans. When time permits, I also record messages to be played for the students with directions for their activities and descriptions of their assignments. Hearing my voice lets them know I am thinking about them and encourages them to do their best in my absence.

Another teacher with many English language learners in her class uses podcasts as a way to enable her students to revisit her lessons after they have been delivered. In class, the teacher presents the lessons live—without the aid of any technology. Then, once the school day is over she creates a quick podcast in which she highlights the major points raised during the face-to-face class meeting. This way, students with access to a computer at home, a school computer lab, or a library can access her podcast before or after school. Her English learners benefit from being able to go back and listen to the podcasts before exams. This way, they are able to hear the lesson numerous times before being assessed on the content.

SMART Boards

Chalkboards and whiteboards are being replaced by interactive, computer-driven whiteboards commonly referred to as SMART Boards. These teaching and learning tools enable a teacher to incorporate Web technology, archive classroom presentations and notes, print notes, and post lessons to the Web for later access. Though still quite expensive, SMART Board technologies continue to improve—and prices continue to drop. While SMART Boards are not available to every teacher, you may be able to reserve one to use on occasion with your students. With the AirLiner slate, you can interact with the Smart Board from anywhere in the room within 52 feet.

ONLINE RESOURCES FOR TEACHERS

There are a host of online resources to help you locate high-quality lesson plans and instructional materials on a variety of topics with applications for English learners. Box 7.2 presents a few sites to get you started. Though the sites presented in this section do not represent a complete listing of sites for teachers, they are proven sites that have been around for some time. As such, the URLs for these sites are unlikely to change over time, and the resources found at these sites have proven worthy to us.

Box 7.2   Sample Online Resources for Teachers

Blue Web'n

Blue Web'n is a collection of peer-reviewed lesson plans and instructional materials organized by subject, grade level, and format (tools, references, lessons, hotlists, resources, tutorials, activities, projects, and more). The lesson plans are chosen by Education Advocates, professionals with advanced degrees and years of experience in education and/or library science. Go to www.filamentality.com/wired/bluewebn/index.cfm, then click on the "Foreign Language" subject area. From there, simply scroll through the results and click on the sites that seem most useful to you.

4Teachers.org

This site features lesson plans and instructional materials and works to help teachers integrate technology into their classrooms. It helps teachers locate and create Web lessons, quizzes, rubrics, and classroom calendars. There are also tools for student use. There is an entire section called "Bilingual Education and ELL," which might be especially helpful as you search for resources to use with your English learners: 4teachers.org/profdev/index.php?profdevid=bee& PHPSESSID=49d9e7ef0d86797d9623116878ff4a86.

Dave's ESL Café

Created by Dave Sperling, this site hosts teacher and student forums and many helpful resources for English learners. Dave's ESL Café has long been a popular Web site used by teachers from all over the world. The student section features pages for a help center, hint of the day, idioms, phrasal verbs, and pronunciation. It can be found at www.eslcafe.com.

The Internet TESL Journal

This site posts articles, teaching techniques, lesson plans, online activities for students, commonly used acronyms, conversation questions, games, and online textbook material. You'll find grammar and vocabulary quizzes, crossword puzzles, and podcasts. The journal, with contributions from many teachers, contains ideas with handouts for students at all grade and proficiency levels. Check monthly for new postings at http://iteslj.org.

PROMOTING CRITICAL THINKING

Software continues to support the development of critical thinking. For development of chronology, Tom Snyder's TimeLiner provides students with the ability to create annotated time lines. The makers of the program Inspiration continue to upgrade software for brainstorming and sequencing information. Map-making programs are also available. There is software that will enable you to give online quizzes and take surveys. Online resources provide simulations and virtual field trips. We now look at some of the latest interactive technology, including blogging, interactive slide presentations, and visual ranking to involve students in higher-level thinking activities.

Blogging

Blogging is beginning to replace dialogue journals as a tool due to its ease of use and the ability to accommodate multiple users. Blogging is the process by which the user creates a Web site with entries made in a journal style and displayed in a reverse chronological order. In the classroom, blogging allows for students to post and for teachers to respond in real time and at any location with Internet connectivity. One of the best ways to develop and assess critical thinking skills is to have students write. And with blogs, students are often excited to begin writing, since blogging provides them with an engaging and nonthreatening writing medium. Some sites, such as eBlog.com, are free, take fewer than five minutes to set up, and can be restricted to invited users. However, educational blogs should be set up with issues of safety and protecting personal identity in mind. When establishing a blog, school names and students' last names should be avoided. Check with your school district on acceptable use policies.

English learners can use blogs in a variety of ways. As a constantly available writing space that can be created in mere minutes, a blog can be a great way to simply get students writing. English learners will gain fluency as writers when they are motivated to keep on writing. The mere fact that blogging is a novel way to have students write should serve as a powerful motivating force for your students.

Class blogs can also serve as a tool for a classroom language exchange. In this situation, learners from different schools, classes, or countries could have access to the blog. The entire exchange would then be available to all readers and could be followed and commented on by others—students, parents, and friends.

Slide Presentation Software

There are many types of slide presentation software that allow students to demonstrate what they have learned. PowerPoint is one of the most commonly found in school districts. As a culminating activity for a unit of study, students can present results of research or an experiment with a slide show that includes graphics and pictures as well as text. English learners can be active participants in team projects with the responsibility of creating slides to include in a presentation. English learners can practice ahead of time which slides they will be responsible for presenting.

If you are already comfortable with creating PowerPoint presentations, you might consider adding audio by recording narration. Add audio and/or video to your existing PowerPoint presentations using a downloadable piece of software called Articulate Presenter: http://www.articulate.com/presenter.html#.

Articulate Presenter lets nontechnical users add narration and interactivity to a standard PowerPoint file. At the press of the button, your presentation is transformed into a compelling Flash-based presentation. (Flash is a popular format for presenting animations on the Web.)

Interactive Software

To quickly assess student achievement and student opinion, teachers are using interactive software. Students are given "clickers" or wireless response systems to indicate yes/no, true/false, or select a response from multiple-choice questions or prompts. TurningPoint and Interwrite PRS (Personal Response System) are two that we are familiar with. Teachers incorporate this interactive feature into their PowerPoint presentations to engage students and quickly check for comprehension. This nonverbal assessment is great to use with English learners. All students enjoy the immediate feedback they receive in a pictorial form of a graph or chart.

Visual Ranking Tools

Visual ranking programs, such as the one developed by Intel Education, requires students to evaluate and rank-order a list of items. Using software, students demonstrate their understanding by prioritizing a list of items. This is an easy way for English learners to participate in the classroom. There is also the capability to input the reason behind their decision making. Finally, their rankings are compared with those of other students in a visual diagram. English learners with minimal productive skills can show evidence of higher-level thinking using this tool.

Digital Photography

The increasing availability of digital cameras, both still and video, offers students additional ways to be creative in conducting research and presenting their results. In science, for example, they can capture the growth of plants and incorporate the pictures into a report. In social studies, students with digital cameras can capture events as they occur, such as interviews or public events, or they can produce skits for later viewing. Photography is highly engaging for students. Beginning English learners can label items in their pictures, while more proficient students can write paragraphs or essays about the subjects in their photos to improve their writing skills and connect with their community. For even more ideas on how to use digital cameras in the classroom, check out this page from Kathy Schrok's Web site: http://school.discovery.com/schrockguide/gadgets.html.

Using Web Sites for Research

With teacher guidance, students can use the Internet as a source of reference information. They can access and/or download text, pictures, graphs, and charts for use in reports or pictures to illustrate stories. They can also communicate with others throughout the Internet.

But remember, as a classroom teacher you are encouraged to closely examine the accuracy of information found on any Web site (Cassutto, 2000; Schrock, 2002, Street, 2005c). It is also a good use of instructional time to teach students *how* to evaluate Web resources (Schrock, 2002; Street, 2005c; Wilhelm, 2004). Many checklists exist for both students and teachers to download and use to evaluate Web sites (Schrock, 2002; Wilhelm, 2004). The Web sites highlighted in this chapter should provide you with many excellent ways to guide students through technology-based lessons. Kathy Shrock's Guide to Educators has evaluation surveys at the elementary, middle, and secondary school levels. There are also evaluations for blogs and podcasts. These easy-to-use, student-friendly forms are found at http://school.discovery.com/schrockguide/eval.html.

New interactive projects, such as WebQuests, are announced all the time for use in a variety of content areas with students of all grades. Students are presented with a question and use the Internet to find the answer in inquiry-based learning activities. They spend time involved in higher-level thinking skills synthesizing, analyzing, and evaluating information rather than searching for it. San Diego State University supports a WebQuest portal at webquest.sdsu.edu. This one-stop site will provide you with the latest and greatest information on WebQuests. And even better, the site is updated regularly by Bernie Dodge, one of founders who is credited with developing WebQuest in 1995.

The JASON Project is a nationally known math, science, and technology program with an extensive Web site. This program was founded by Robert Ballard, explorer and oceanographer known for discovering the wreck of the *Titanic*. Each year, students follow the scientists in their work all over the world through virtual field trips and become part of the research community.

Internet Simulations

For years, students have participated in the Stock Market Game, a "real-life" simulation of investment endorsed by the National Council for Economic Education. Students compete against other teams and invest an initial $100,000 in common stocks during a 10-week trading session. Students learn about the U.S. economy as they execute the steps to buy and sell shares of stock, select criteria for evaluating a business, identify different forms of business, and find the sources of funds available to these businesses. There are other stock market games and other simulations available. Check with teachers at your school for additional ideas.

The significance of using the latest technologies in the classroom is that they support the delivery of content in all curriculum areas if selected for the appropriate grade level. The virtual manipulation of objects and information allows students to proceed at the appropriate academic level when language skills may be below level. Interactive software emphasizes receptive skills (listening and reading) rather than productive skills. The Internet provides an instant source of information to students in a variety of languages. There are also Web sites for translations, though they should be used cautiously, because the translation technologies available today are far from perfect. The Google Language Tools (http://www.google.com/language_tools) are worth trying out.

Virtual Field Trips

In order to provide background information and visual references, teachers use virtual field trips with their students. With a one-computer classroom or a computer lab, students have opportunities to see places that are far away or perhaps logistically difficult to visit. Using virtual field trips, teachers can quickly provide English learners with needed background knowledge and examples of concepts. In addition, with virtual field trips, students can revisit as often as they want! Though virtual field trips are not commonplace today, futurists are projecting that they will become quite common by 2020 (2020 Visions, n.d.).

BENEFITS OF USING TECHNOLOGY WITH ENGLISH LEARNERS

As your resources and individual experiences with technology increase, you will find many ways to integrate technology-related lessons in your classroom. Explore how you can make use of television, telephone, audio and visual recordings, photography, and software programs and Web sites available to you today. Box 7.3 lists the many benefits for English learners.

Box 7.3   Benefits of Using Technology in the Classroom With English Learners

Depending on your choice of technology and activities, your students' technology-related lessons will

☐ Engage and motivate students

☐ Involve students actively, individually or with a partner

☐ Build background knowledge

☐ Use receptive rather than productive skills

☐ Give immediate feedback

☐ Promote higher-level thinking skills

☐ Pair students with experts

☐ Provide an authentic audience

☐ Offer immediate reference material

☐ Stimulate creativity

☐ Develop skills and comprehension, allowing for repetition and reinforcement

☐ Support word processing

☐ Enable students to have virtual experiences that would otherwise be unavailable

☐ Provide ways to publish student work

☐ Provide assessment tools

Technology provides students with access to or opens students' eyes to the four "I's" of information, images, interaction, and inquiry" (Pollack, 2007, p. 102). We hope that the strategies presented in this chapter will give you many ideas to try in your own classroom. Remember, you are not alone. Chapter 8 discusses other resources that are available to you and how to involve others in the classroom.

SUGGESTED ACTIVITIES

1. Select a topic of study and identify all the technologies you could incorporate into the lesson to help your English learners.

2. Evaluate where your students are in their development of technology skills. Plan a technology-related lesson that will offer them the opportunity to use their skills as they become involved with the content you are presenting.

3. Research Web sites that would offer valuable support for your students. As one example, visit www.eslcafe.com to access Dave Sperling's Web site, Dave's ESL Café. Visit or join a forum on elementary or secondary education.

4. Make plans to get specialized training in instructional technology in order to develop other ways that you can capitalize on various media to support your teaching efforts.

5. Using a free online dictionary, such as Yahoo! Dictionary, choose some words that might prove difficult for your English learners to pronounce. Demonstrate for your students how to use the online dictionary, focusing on the online pronunciation feature. Let your students experiment with the online dictionary and have them reflect on whether the pronunciation feature of this site proved helpful.

CHAPTER EIGHT

Involving Others

"It's not a globe, it's a balloon," said one student to another. "Let me show you how to blow it up."

When the teacher heard that statement, she realized she was not the only person from whom her students would be learning English. There would be many "helping teachers" who would introduce new concepts, model pronunciation, and make corrections when necessary.

Because children learn as much English, if not more, from their peers as they do from the planned curriculum, teachers can capitalize on this natural phenomenon in systematic ways. This chapter will highlight many of the ways you can utilize the resources of other people—from children in the classroom and school personnel to people in the community—in efforts to facilitate language acquisition.

PEER INSTRUCTION

Sometimes teachers forget that some of the most significant learning that takes place in school is neither in the classroom nor mediated by professional educators. You only have to think back to your own learning experiences that had the most impact to recall that most of them occurred on the playground, in the lunchroom, during hall passing, and mostly during supposed playtime with friends and schoolmates. Often these were lessons about sharing, friendship, and loyalty, but occasionally they covered the realities of betrayal, intimidation, and fear. In any case, there is little doubt that age mates and peer pressure often have considerably more influence on student behavior than do the best intentions of teachers.

It is a wise teacher who recognizes the power of peer interactions and seeks to capitalize on this influence to promote learning objectives. As an example, when a tenth-grade student is asked his favorite class in school, he doesn't even hesitate to reply, "Spanish."

"Spanish?"

"Kinda surprised, aren't you?" he replies with a grin.

This boy is an athlete and is not known for his academic interests. Puzzled, you investigate further, asking him to elaborate. What you discover is that he absolutely loves Spanish class because the teacher gives kids the opportunity to talk to each other, if they can manage to do so using Spanish and a modified sign language.

For any number of reasons, children often learn best from one another, especially in situations when they don't feel critically judged. After all, where do kids learn about life's most important lessons—such as sex, love, and friendship—except from one another? And where else do they learn about language?

Buddy System

In order to help new students feel comfortable, one obvious structure is to assign a designated partner as a guide to aid adjustment. This helper is ideally positioned to give encouragement and to make sure the student has the right supplies and follows directions given to the class. Of equal importance, the new arrival will have a companion, someone to interact with throughout the day. In addition, "buddies" also profit from their experience as helpers. They learn what it means to be responsible in carrying through commitments. Their relationships with the teacher will be enhanced as they realize they were selected (or volunteered) for this responsibility. They learn the joy of explaining things to others in a way the others finally understand. In fact, many of us were "born" as teachers when we were given opportunities as children to help our peers and siblings. Many of us can recall what a privilege it was to be chosen to escort another student to the office! Not only were we the ones chosen from the entire class, but we were also released from the discipline codes of "Stay in your seat," and "No talking."

Studies of conversations show that children are quite different from teachers when they point out mistakes to their peers. Children focus on the social aspect, asking for clarification only when they cannot understand what is communicated. Teachers, however, attend to the content and language, rectify the mistake, and expect the child to use the correct response in the future. This, of course, can be a humiliating experience for children who are trying hard to please a new teacher in a new culture. One obvious example of this occurs when assignments are read aloud. Children who are struggling to pronounce a word are quite grateful for the assistance of a peer, yet when the teacher corrects them, they often feel censored.

With elementary students, another approach is to assign different buddies for different tasks. This widens the exposure of students without overwhelming any single individual. For example, one student might be assigned as a "study buddy," a second student would function as a "lunch buddy" to take the student to the cafeteria, and a third student would be a "bus buddy" to make sure the student gets on the right bus and has a person to sit with.

Each of the helpers is given an opportunity to develop a sense of responsibility and leadership skills. The experience also helps each buddy develop empathy, as he or she feels the experience of one who is different. With each assistant the teacher recruits, he or she is also able to create a new bond in the ongoing relationship with students. It is as if the teacher is saying, "I trust you. I value your help. I feel grateful for your willingness to pitch in and help. We are all trying to learn together."

TEAM TEACHING

Rarely are you the only teacher a student comes in contact with during the day. Integrating the curriculum across disciplines is extremely helpful for English learners, for several reasons.

Thematic learning supports language development and academic content (Houk, 2005). It offers students repeated opportunity to hear a group of words. Teachers can work together to target principles of grammar. Furthermore, repetition reinforces concepts. You can develop your own themes or use commercially prepared kits, in which English and social studies skills are combined with science and math concepts.

Although it might be optimistic to expect all the teachers to coordinate their efforts, it may be more practical to coordinate intentions with a few with whom you have established rapport. For example, an elementary teacher can make sure that the librarian and art teacher are aware of what has been taking place and what they can do to help. Even the bus driver can be recruited to pitch in: "When Tasha comes on the bus, ask her slowly how her day was. Then please make sure she does not sit alone."

Many schools are now implementing teaming or are providing teachers with coordinated planning time and shared students structured into their schedules. Most important, secondary teachers must communicate with one another on a regular basis so that progress is not restricted to a single class or compartmentalized in such a way that the student becomes confused with inconsistencies or overwhelmed by vocabulary. For example, a social studies teacher can work with a math teacher to reinforce the concept of angles in studying the pyramids of ancient Egypt. On a more general level, several teachers can get together and coordinate their efforts: "I notice that Ling really cringes when I attempt to talk to him individually. How do you approach him? Maybe we could all try a consistent approach."

Imagine how frustrated an English learner would be if she were told by one teacher to do or say one thing, while another required something else, and still another quite another thing. For example, a student is encouraged by one teacher to talk as much as possible and not worry about grammar; another teacher tells him to exercise more restraint and speak only after he has thought through what he wants to say and how he will say it; a third teacher absolutely insists that he not speak at all until he can "talk right." With these mixed messages, such a student is likely to follow the advice of the third teacher, avoiding the risk of making mistakes whenever possible.

At one urban high school, the teachers make a committed effort to work together and share the responsibility for educating all students. With a large English learner population, the faculty wanted to ensure that all students were able to read critically and write well. In order to meet these worthy goals, the teachers examined and agreed upon a set of seven literacy strategies.

Each teacher, regardless of content area, took the time to teach the seven strategies to all their students, and the results were impressive. When students moved from one subject to another, they encountered the same seven literacy strategies—all of which were designed to improve the students' academic language skills, something that current research suggests is crucial for English learners if they are to master challenging content (Bielenberg & Wong-Fillmore, 2005; Cummins, 1986; Lachat, 2004; Scarcella, 2003; Zwiers, 2004). For example, students were using reflective writing in math, engaging in shared reading in history, creating concept maps in biology, and using reciprocal teaching in English. Schoolwide collaboration is difficult to achieve—especially at the middle and high school levels—but when it is successful, it can really pay huge dividends for students.

SCHOOL PERSONNEL

There may be additional resource people available in your school or in your district for collaboration. One such specialist is the English language development teacher. Generally, nonproficient children are placed in an English language development class for part of the day and in the regular classroom for the rest of the time. The number of hours varies depending on the school district and the needs of the students. The dynamics of the English language development class may be far different from the way you might usually structure your own class.

You may be able to coordinate with the English language development teacher on the vocabulary of the subject you teach. Another approach is for the English language development teacher to use sheltered English to teach material or skills in the content area. If you contact the English language development teacher and correlate your classroom teaching lessons, he or she can prepare the student by introducing needed background concepts before you present new material in your class. In addition, the English language development teacher can introduce related vocabulary. If you notice mistakes in grammar or pronunciation, you can communicate them to this teacher, who can work with the student individually, allowing you to address other matters. By coordinating your efforts, you will eliminate duplication and avoid subjecting the student to undue academic pressure. This teacher may also be able to support your lessons with reinforcement and individual practice.

Although being placed in English development classes offers special instruction and an opportunity to meet with like peers, it also has some disadvantages. Students often complain that they don't like being identified as different. Pulling them out of their regular classrooms may make them feel as if they are falling even further behind or missing shared experiences with the other students. Furthermore, they are limited in hearing English as spoken by their peers. It is helpful to be aware of the awkward situation these students find themselves in and the mixed emotions they experience.

Again, coordinating with other professionals can help to minimize some of these problems. For example, you might say, "I notice that Hassan leaves class reluctantly when it is time to meet with you. It seems as if he does not want to make up more work that he missed. If in your work with him you could combine some of my tasks with your own, he would not feel as reluctant."

Other possible sources of support are bilingual teachers, foreign language teachers, and English teachers in your school or in your district. They might be willing to share strategies and materials with you, or you could invite them to visit your classroom to observe and make suggestions for identified students. Outside the classroom, you could ask them to help you brainstorm strategies to use in delivering specific content.

If a student receives a reading score below the grade level on a standardized test, the student is entitled to help from a reading resource teacher. Once again, rather than have the reading teacher work in isolation from the regular classroom, you can discuss your units with the reading teacher so that he or she can prepare the student to participate in the regular classroom. This professional will be dealing not only with reading skills per se, but also with writing, speaking, and listening. The student can practice with the reading teacher privately before being called on in front of a group of peers or the whole class.

Traditionally, the reading teacher has worked with students in a "pull-out" situation in a room outside the regular classroom. However, rather than isolating students, reading teachers are beginning to work right in the regular classroom. This provides the reading teacher with the opportunity to see how the regular classroom, and the teacher in particular, functions. It is also less disruptive for the students, who are often afraid (rightfully so) they are going to miss something "fun" or "important" when they are called out of class.

Special education teachers can also be a resource. They have experience in making modifications for students. They can help you determine if reduced assignments or extra time for testing would be in order. They may suggest calculator usage or word processing as an aid. They may help you with physical changes in the classroom, such as preferential seating, and can help you develop behavior plans based on the actions of the students. They may also have resources to help you, such as talking board pictures. They can also help you determine when structural approaches are helpful. For example, one special education teacher notes:

> I had two Vietnamese students who were having trouble with conversational phrases. They could memorize them but did not use them. So, I sat down with them and explained the parts of speech—subjects and predicates. Then, the girls were able to make connections with their own languages and quickly mastered the phrases.

Other personnel to consult with would include the school counselor, social worker, and psychologist. They can offer aid in the areas of handling adjustment, building self-esteem, and establishing support groups. They can also deal with issues related to fear of failure, perfectionist attitudes, and other cognitive messages that interfere with learning.

In one application of counseling theory called "cognitive interventions," students are taught to monitor their internal thinking processes and change the way they talk to themselves inside their heads. If a student says to herself, "I'm stupid" every time she makes a mistake, this is going to be very inhibiting to her learning English—or anything else. Instead of being so hard on herself, she can be taught to substitute, "I'm human and I only made a mistake." Some other examples are as follows:

What a Student Thinks	Alternative Thoughts
"I am the only one who has problems."	"Others are struggling as well."
"This is *awful* that I messed up."	"This is only a minor setback."
"This *should* be easy."	"This is a real challenge for me."
"I'll *never* get this stupid language."	"I will learn English in time."

In addition, counselors can help you work directly with students in addressing emotional needs. We often forget to look at the big picture, how struggles with schoolwork and language skills affect every other facet of a child's life. When needed, referrals can be made to other resources in the community.

For example, in the case of one child who was struggling not only with learning English but also with staying out of the reach of his alcoholic, abusive father, a school counselor was instrumental in helping to stabilize the family situation. Efforts by the principal, school psychologist, counselor, and referring teacher were all united in their determination to help this child succeed in spite of adverse conditions.

When this child was later able to express himself more fully, he explained to his teacher that as much as he appreciated the help he received with his school performance and language abilities, of even greater importance was the interaction that helped change the poisonous atmosphere of his home. If these American people seemed to care enough to intervene on his behalf, surely he could learn their language so that he might thank them.

One last group of school personnel who offer a specialized area of expertise are the speech teachers. They can offer suggestions related to pronunciation, but remember, for some students, it will be difficult to speak a new language without an accent if they are above the age of 12 or 13 when they begin to learn. Some students will never lose their accents.

CROSS-AGE TUTORING

Another type of project that has met with success is a tutoring program. As older and experienced students are paired with younger students, benefits to both parties accrue. For students who have recently arrived in this country, there is much comfort in meeting someone who can identify with the experience of being immersed in a new culture and who understands how problems arise. Older students can empathize and share what they did and how it helped them. They also serve as role models. One such program might involve setting up a system whereby junior high or high school students meet once a week with early elementary school students. The older students are given the responsibility to plan for and prepare an hour of activity.

Tutoring sessions require coordination by both teachers. For example, the older students can be responsible for implementing activities related to a unit being studied in the regular classroom. Students might work in groups or be paired individually. Their activities might include reading to younger children, sight word instruction, or word puzzles. Hearing-sound activities can include reading Dr. Seuss's books to attain phonemic awareness. Letter-sound activities can involve putting up letters for a known word and changing the first letter (*run* to *sun* to *fun*). Writing activities can include writing books or letters together. The tutors, under the supervision of the teachers, would have to decide what activities would be appropriate, which materials they would need, and how to structure the time spent with the students.

This presents a problem-solving situation that involves higher-level thinking skills for the tutors. The tutors would have to analyze their own learning and break it down into steps for the younger students. These activities would serve also as a reinforcement for the older students. The tutors thus find themselves in a new role, as "teacher," which provides them with experience to help their own children in the future as they grow up.

They can also tutor students who are learning their native language. For example, Spanish speakers can work with native English-speaking students who are learning Spanish as an additional language. They can help with grammar as well as lessons on elements of culture. As peer models, the Spanish speakers can provide opportunities for other students to interact with native speakers. As another benefit, it may also serve as an introduction to a career in education.

The younger, less proficient students are placed in situations that are enjoyable and meaningful and that have low pressure. Remember, language is social in nature. In a tutoring situation, students are free to analyze their language skills and share strategies with each other. The older students can develop a sense of pride and accomplishment from helping others that can lead to an increase in self-esteem and the development of positive attitudes about themselves and school. Studies show (Allen, 2000) that tutors gain in achievement and attitude, giving credence to the idea, "If you want to learn something, teach it!"

PARENTS AND FAMILIES

It is especially important for families to be involved in activities that support literacy. Teachers can provide parents and child care givers with examples of and instructions for activities they can do at home. Many districts offer programs for parents during the day and in the evenings. Schools frequently have extended library hours for parents to check out books. Reading to young children in any language and talking about the reading are vital activities that support fluency of communication. Those parents who are literate, but not in English, can be encouraged to read to their children in their native language. Teachers can impress on parents their responsibility to pass their heritage (folk tales, rhymes, and poetry) from one generation to the next.

Outreach

Many schools are developing programs to invite parents and families into the schools as well as go out into the community. Schools often host a variety of workshops and training for families. Information sessions cover parent conferences, how to interpret test scores, services offered by the school, and rights of parents to accept or refuse services for their children. Parents need to know how to find out the school boundaries, how to arrange for bus transportation, how to obtain the school year calendar, and what to do if the student is absent or will be leaving school early.

Counselors and teachers may lead a variety of programs, from how to help students with homework, to how to apply for college, to how to understand child development. Teacher teams or subject area departments may host programs dedicated to their subject area, such as family geography night, math night, or literacy night. Most schools hold a fall program, such as "Back to School Night," to introduce teachers to families and a spring program, such as "Open House" to display student accomplishments.

The Anaheim Union High School District in Anaheim, California, sends a "classroom on wheels," a bus with laptops, into the community to offer classes on literacy and computer skills for parents along with other resources. The Santa Ana Unified School District in Santa Ana, California, developed Padres Promotores de la Educación, which trains volunteer parents to provide other parents in the community with information on school services and higher education. They conduct community meetings and make home visits. Find out what programs your district offers and help make your students' families aware of them.

There are many ways to reach out to parents. Other ideas include developing a list of community resources and services, ways and means to volunteer, and support groups for parents (Epstein et al., 2002). Perhaps your parent-teacher association or parent-teacher organization has already begun family involvement programs in your school. Box 8.1 highlights a number of professional organizations that provide free resources for parents and for teachers.

Box 8.1   Online Resources for Parents and Families

International Reading Association

The International Reading Association has a section of their Web site called "Parent Resources." Many of the booklets, brochures, videos, DVDs, and other resources are available for free in both English and Spanish (reading.org/resources/tools/parent.html).

The National Association for Multicultural Education

The National Association for Multicultural Education provides many useful resources for parents (www.nameorg.org/resources/parents.html).

The National Council of Teachers of English

The National Council of Teachers of English is a helpful organization when it comes to locating information of interest to parents (www .ncte.org/parents?source=gs).

CT Parents Plus

CT Parents Plus is Connecticut's Parent Information and Resource Center. This site describes how teachers and parents of children receiving benefits from Title I funds will work together to improve student achievement and meet the needs of students (www.ctparents plus.org/tipsheets/SchoolParentCompact.asp).

Teachers can also explain to parents how children learn, as well as the type of behavior expected in the classroom. The problem is that teachers receive so little training in how to consult with parents. What do you do with a parent who is resistant to your best efforts? How do you handle the parent who feels you are meddling? What do you do when there are obvious family problems that are affecting the child's behavior? How do you get parents to comply with what you are suggesting?

In an ideal situation, counseling specialists would be available to address these difficulties. Alas, such help is not often available, leaving you with the task. Because you may feel unprepared to apply advanced-level helping skills, you can recruit the assistance of experts to help train you and others who are interested as resources

(Kottler & Kottler, 2007). University faculty can recommend books for you to read and can design workshops for you in this area that will teach you strategies to use in consulting with parents.

In one school, a teacher who was taking some counseling classes put together a mini-workshop for parents who were interested in augmenting their skills in parenting. These sessions ran four weeks at a time and covered such topics as opening lines of communication with your child, setting limits, balancing school and outside activities, and when to seek outside help for family problems. Consider collaborating with other helping professionals in your school to involve parents and families in your students' education.

INTERGENERATIONAL TUTORING

Two groups of individuals may be available to work individually to support your students in the classroom. Check with your administration with regards to policies and procedures for using volunteers in the classroom.

Senior Citizens

Adults of retirement age are able to offer a wealth of skills and knowledge. Many cultures value group interaction. Intergenerational tutoring is an extension that naturally fits into the public school arena. There are many parents and grandparents who will volunteer their time to help students. Also, they can read to students or have students read to them. They can offer explanations or translations as appropriate. They can do demonstrations and give additional examples for individuals or small groups. The teacher needs only to match the adult with the student and provide appropriate activities.

University Students

Another resource that may be just around the corner is university students. They often have flexible time to be available during the school day or for afterschool sessions. In particular, university students who are curious about or are pursuing a teaching career will be interested in spending time in your classroom. They are encouraged, if not required, to have extended experiences observing and working with young people. They can help supervise activities, monitor assignments, and provide individual support. Bilingual university students not only provide important role models of those obtaining higher education in various fields, but also they can offer primary language support to English learners. Look to them to help your students express problems they are experiencing or concerns they have.

COMMUNITY RESOURCES

Open the doors to your classroom. Venture out or bring the world inside your room to provide immediate experiences for your students. Anyone who has become truly fluent in another language did not learn it in the classroom. Once you get students excited about learning English, they will be motivated to take what they have learned into the real world, where it really counts.

As with most learning, motivation is a key. If students see a reason why mastering English is one key to life satisfaction and success, your only job will be to structure their learning, because wild horses couldn't hold them back. If you have ever traveled in a foreign country where you couldn't communicate your basic needs, it did not take much incentive for you to learn, "Where is the toilet?" People have a habit of learning what they need most to get what they want.

Field Trips

Expand the classroom by taking a field trip to a farm, factory, or post office. For some students, the bus ride through the community alone is an eye-opening experience. You would be surprised how many students have never left their neighborhoods.

Visiting restaurants of different ethnic groups is a popular field trip. Decor, food, background music, and in some cases foreign menus give students an indication of different customs. Visiting museums to see traveling exhibitions can also be a worthwhile trip. It is important for all students to see contributions made by people of diverse backgrounds.

Arrange for your students to go into the community to inform, entertain, or engage in service learning projects. This will provide students with authentic audiences to make their experiences meaningful and relevant. Students will learn about others, develop their social skills, meet new people, and gain new perspectives. You promote cross-cultural understanding and help build a sense of community in your area.

Visitors

There are many people in the local area who may be willing to visit your classroom. Invite businesspeople to come and demonstrate the services they provide or the products they produce, as they relate to topics of study, to bring these subjects alive for the students. The subject of owning a business can be a lesson in itself. Many people will bring samples of their products for the students. The visit can serve as an introductory or culminating activity for a unit. Students can prepare a list of questions ahead of time. Homemakers have talents or hobbies as well that they can share with your students. Asking members of your students' families to talk about their work or avocation will create bonds in the classroom. You don't have to wait for Career Day or Culture Day. Integrate these visits into your curriculum.

Imagine a renowned chef coming to class bearing samples of the masterpieces she has created, letting the children taste her treats, and explaining how she creates new dishes. Then, she describes her own life story, how when she first arrived in this country and stepped off the boat, she could not speak a word of English.

She says she felt as if she were invisible, that as long as she could not speak the language of this country, nobody would give her a chance. She was determined, however, that she would speak English like a native (the kids laugh because she has a thick accent). "Okay, okay, so I don't speak so good." (The kids laugh again.) "Well, I don't speak well. Better? Anyway, English is everything to be successful. What good is it to cook like an angel if I can't talk to other people? All of you, not just those of you from other countries, must study hard in school. Your whole life, people will judge you by the way you speak." What an effective presentation that would be!

Artists, musicians, skilled craftspeople, and scientists could present their work to students of any level. Contact the various agencies and institutions in your vicinity to see if they have a speakers' bureau from which you can request presenters who were former English learners for your students.

On the secondary level, for more proficient students, you can consider inviting guests to talk about their personal experiences on key concepts, such as acculturation, immigration, prejudice, political power, and social conditions in our society. Again, they can share their unique stories and contributions to our society.

Contact local businesses and industries for speakers. Many employers will support their employees volunteering their time in schools. Some will have formal mentoring programs that you will be able to have your students participate in.

CULTURAL EXCHANGE PROGRAMS

Art, music, dress, and foods can be the central themes of a multicultural awareness experience. Potluck lunches or dinners bring together people of the community. Students can be assigned to give an informative talk, sing a song, demonstrate a dance, explain a game, write a recipe, or prepare a dish. Students or adults can show pictures or slides of places they have lived or traveled and talk about the customs there.

Perhaps you can take your students to community festivals, cultural exhibits, or cultural performances. Another idea is to invite students on semester exchange programs to visit your classrooms. There are many ways to foster cultural exchanges.

LANGUAGE FOR ALL

Although this book emphasizes teaching strategies for individuals with differences in their language capacities, children are very similar in their basic desires. They want to understand the world around them. They want to be accepted and liked by their peers. They want to develop skills and knowledge that will help them be successful in life. They want to feel validated by their teachers. Through the strategies presented in this book, it is possible for teachers to be more sensitive to the children in their care.

In spite of your best intentions to be more responsive to children who are struggling as newcomers to our culture and language, there are limits on the time, energy, and resources that you have available. Even though you may be overburdened with other responsibilities and priorities, even though you don't feel adequately prepared to handle many of the challenges you will face with English learners, you can make a difference in a relatively short period of time.

SUGGESTED ACTIVITIES

1. To expand student experiences, create a list of possible guest speakers with culturally diverse backgrounds to present to your students and develop a list of potential field trip sites to take your students out of the classroom.

2. Plan an integrated interdisciplinary unit with a colleague. Collaborate on objectives, instructional strategies, and assessments.

3. List possible resource personnel in your school or district with whom you could consult on individual student progress.

4. Research Web sites for information on developing partnerships with families to improve literacy.

5. Learn some basic counseling skills (such as "active listening") in order to sensitize yourself better to nuances in expressed communication and to respond more effectively to students' emotional needs.

CHAPTER NINE

Putting It All Together

The concepts and skills presented in this book provide you with some of the basics you need to implement structures and programs helpful to the students in your classroom who are struggling the most. Now it is time to put together everything we covered into some sort of organized framework.

Recent research on brain functioning as it relates to learning is one useful integrative model. We begin with a review of the brain research that relates in particular to working with English learners in the classroom, offer general guidelines to help get you started, and end with a lesson plan format for you to follow.

CLASSROOM IMPLICATIONS OF BRAIN RESEARCH

Educators have been following closely the results of current brain research to see how they can make use of new findings. New technologies, such as magnetic resonance imaging, positron emission tomography, and magnetoencephalography, to name a few, have increased our knowledge of how the brain functions. When this is added to recent advances in the understanding of neurotransmitters and brain chemistry, a clearer picture has emerged of how the brain learns.

Findings may be summarized as follows (Sousa, 2004):

• *Past experience affects new learning.* It is important to activate prior knowledge before introducing new concepts. This means using the students' experiences as examples of what you teach.

• *The brain is always changing based on new experiences.* This process is known as *neuroplasticity*. Teachers should provide educational experiences that will be somewhat challenging yet not too frustrating for students (Caulfield, Kidd, & Kocher, 2000).

• *Both sides of the brain are involved in learning.* Although the two hemispheres of the brain are specialized—the left side is logical in orientation, responsible for speech and analytical thinking, whereas the right side is intuitive in orientation, gathering information from images, responding to language through context, and processing information abstractly and holistically—people learn best when both hemispheres are involved. Lessons should be designed to include both verbal and visual concepts, to present both logical and intuitive concepts, and to give students options in terms of assessments that enable them to demonstrate what they know in a way that reflects their individual learning styles.

• *A positive classroom environment promotes learning.* Students need to feel comfortable in the classroom and to feel that they can express their opinions and have them respected. In order for this process to occur, you must take the time to build a trusting relationship with your students and help them develop into a community of learners based on respect for each other.

• *Emotion plays a vital role in learning.* Once students are comfortable, if they like and are excited about what they learn, endorphins are produced. As a result, student interest will be maintained, and they will remember things more easily. They will also tend to move toward higher levels of thinking—analysis, synthesis, and evaluation. Novelty and humor play important roles in engaging students. Involvement and interaction are critical. Remember, as well, that lecturing is the least effective method to use in relation to students' retention of material.

• *Students will respond differently based on their sensory preferences.* Teachers need to provide experiences to address all sensory preferences and learning styles. In large classes, this is a very challenging task, considering all the other things that teachers must attend to. That doesn't mean that it's impossible to individualize learning, only that it is difficult to do so—but we believe it is well worth it.

- *The brain searches for meaning.* English learners need a *lot* of stimuli. As mentioned earlier, the importance of a rich environment and peer interaction cannot be stressed enough.

- *Students can become aware of their thinking processes.* Teach children metacognitive processes so that they become aware of what they know and how they learn. Make time for students to self-monitor their progress.

- *Provide time for reflection.* Allow students a few minutes to review what they have learned. Take "time-outs" of one to three minutes to make sense of what is being presented or learned. Support introspection.

In their review of the literature on effective programs for English learners, Samway and McKeon (1999) identify several indicators that are relevant to you as a classroom teacher. Three stand out in particular. First is establishing high expectations for students. Teachers must maintain their standards of achievement and hold all students accountable (Scarcella, 2003). Second, students need to interact with each other in meaningful ways. Language development occurs with academic development. Third, until conversation is possible, students are allowed to respond in their own language and have it translated when such support is available. These same ideas have been mentioned throughout the book. They are central, for example, to Freeman and Freeman's (1998) *Principles for Success,* presented in Chapter 6.

PLANNING INSTRUCTION AND ASSESSMENT

From classroom to classroom, learning takes place in a variety of ways. Although there is no magic wand to ensure that a smooth and speedy process will take place for your English learners, careful planning and preparation will provide you with the basis on which to structure a positive learning environment in which students will have the opportunity to succeed.

Educational Design

Plan reflectively and strategically what you want to do and how you intend to reach your goals (Dick & Carey, 1990; Wiggins & McTighe, 2005). Several steps are crucial.

Step 1: Determine Your Goals and Objectives

Whatever grade level you teach, from kindergarten through twelfth grade, and whatever subject you teach, from core courses, such as reading, science, mathematics, and social studies, to elective courses, such as vocational or fine arts, you need to identify your goals. Wiggins and McTighe (2005) ask, What are the essential understandings? The big ideas? The sequence of skills? Begin by selecting what you want your students to know and be able to do. Consult your state standards and district frameworks or course syllabi for direction at this starting point.

Then determine what your specific objectives will be, that is, what students should know or be able to do that is observable and measurable. It is the teacher's responsibility to set the direction for learning (Pollock, 2007). Include not only your content and subject area skills but also the academic language and grammar skills.

This is vital when planning lessons for English learners. Though you might not be used to thinking in terms of the language objectives of your lessons, doing so will really help you to design effective lessons for your English learners. For example, the Sheltered Instruction Observation Protocol (SIOP) model (Echevarria, Vogt, & Short, 2004), the Sheltered Approach, and the Specially Designed Academic Instruction in English (SDAIE) approach all stress the importance of examining curriculum from a language perspective. Doing so enables teachers to plan their instruction according to what aspects of English their students will need in order to meet the content objectives of the lesson (Gibbons, 2003). When teachers plan language objectives as well as content objectives, their students benefit.

This is not as difficult as it might seem at first, since the language objectives will quite naturally relate to the key vocabulary, reading, writing, speaking, and listening skills of your lessons. For example, content area teachers can certainly teach content-specific language in their classrooms. A middle school English teacher exploring *Hatchet* by Gary Paulson might present the following language objective: Students will list 10 descriptive words (adjectives) to describe the place where they most enjoy spending time, with the following content objective: Students will analyze the relevance of the setting (e.g., place, time, customs) to the mood, tone, and meaning of the text.

Connecting language objectives with content objectives may seem foreign at first, but once you begin to examine curriculum from a language perspective you'll be amazed at how the language lessons will begin to jump out at you.

Step 2: Select Your Assessment

The next stage is to identify how you will know what your students have learned and to what degree they have mastered the objectives you identified in Step 1. You may need to be creative with the assessments you choose, depending on the level of proficiency of the English learners. Consider offering a choice to students as to how they will demonstrate their knowledge or skill development, or you may even ask them to create the type of assessment. Teachers need to determine what the acceptable evidence of achievement will look like (Pollock, 2007; Wiggins & McTighe, 2005).

In some cases, the traditional paper-and-pencil test will be easy and efficient to implement. However, you may find adaptations to be necessary, such as providing support with vocabulary boxes or adding illustrations. Consider recording the questions for students to follow along as they read and then ask them to indicate true or false or to select the best answer from a multiple-choice list.

Nontraditional forms will more likely be the assessment of choice, especially with beginning English students. For them, a drawing, a sequencing project, or performance may be a more appropriate format. One-on-one interviews may help you best determine whether an understanding of a concept has been met. A list of alternative assessments is found in Box 9.1.

Box 9.1   List of Alternative Assessments

Animated stories, art, annotated bibliographies

Blogs, brochures, bulletin boards

Children's books, collages

Databases, demonstrations, dioramas, drawings

Editorials, experiment results

Fashion shows, fishbowl discussions

Games, graphic organizers

Historical portrayals of person or event

Illustrated time lines, inner-outer circle discussions, interviews

Journal entries

KWL charts

Learning logs, letters, literature circle discussions

Maps, models, movies

Newscasts, newspapers

Obituaries, oral histories

Photographic essays, plays, poems, podcasts, political cartoons, posters

Questionnaires, quilts

Recordings, role plays

Shared readings, simulation, skits, slide shows, songs, speeches, storyboards

Television programs, think-alouds

Unit summaries with illustrations

Video documentaries, virtual field trips, visual-quote activities

Web sites

Xylographs (wood engraving) or other artistic renderings

Yearbooks

Z–A or A–Z alphabet presentations

For performance assessment, consider adding an audience to your classroom. Is there an individual or group with whom it would be appropriate for students to share their knowledge or show their skill development? Consider inviting a guest or guests to class, such as principals, parents, community members, or other students.

Step 3: Assess the Level of Your Students

Determine the entry level of your students. It is critical to determine their content background, previous school experiences, and language development. What prior knowledge and experiences will they need to have in order to be successful? Will you need to build experiences for them before they take on a new topic or begin a new reading? What vocabulary will they need to have before beginning a new concept? If you use a KWL chart, begin the K section. What do students already know, what dispositions do they hold, and/or what skills have they already mastered?

Step 4: Determine the Learning Activities and Instruction

This is where the actual lesson takes place. Now is the time to decide on the methods of instruction you will use and the sequence of activities in which students will have the opportunity to practice new words, concepts, and skills and to apply new ideas. Wolfe (2001) includes in her "toolkit" the following activities:

- *Writing.* To have students refine their thinking by organizing and expressing ideas.
- *Mnemonics.* To help students recall facts and the meaning of terms, such as acrostic sentences and acronyms, rhymes and phrases, keyword mnemonics, and narrative chaining.
- *Peer Teaching.* To have students provide support and a means for social interaction.

Sousa (2004) suggests the following lesson design based on Madeline Hunter's (1982) model. Not all elements will be present in every lesson, but all will likely be included in every unit.

Anticipatory Set. Select a strategy that will get students' attention. It can range from showing a picture to telling a story to something humorous. The anticipatory set establishes the tone for the class period. It should relate to something students are familiar with and the objectives for the lesson.

If your students don't have the prerequisite background knowledge, you may need to "jump-start" or provide an introductory mini-lesson by introducing vocabulary and reviewing concepts, showing pictures, or engaging in simulations or some sort of experiential activity (Echevarria, Vogt, & Short, 2004). Depending on the number of students, you may choose to do this with a small group or with the entire class.

State Objective(s). For English learners, avoid the "educationese" that is sometimes found in content standards. The objectives need to be stated and written simply and clearly. Include the content area objectives and the English language development objectives.

Purpose. Explain why the students need to master the objectives and explain how they relate to prior learning and future learning. Describe the whole picture. Students do not always make the connections on their own and need the teacher to show the links (Echevarria, Vogt, & Short, 2004). This can easily be accomplished by referring to previous activities, reinforcing vocabulary, and by using advance graphic organizers. Include a description of what the assessment will be like so students will know what to focus on.

Input. Provide students with the information they need while addressing as many of the multiple intelligences as possible. This can take place in a variety of ways, from demonstrations, reading, lecture, and audiovisual presentations to student-conducted research, experiments, or presentations.

Modeling. Show students clear examples to help them make sense of the new material. This is especially important for English learners. Modeling provides the scaffolding they need and the language prompts that will enable them to master new content (Echevarria, Vogt, & Short, 2004; Gray & Fleischman, 2004/2005; Scarcella, 2003).

Check for Understanding. Be sure students are making meaning of the new material by implementing any of a variety of techniques, from a "thumbs up, thumbs down" response, audience response technology, question and answer, discussion, a quiz, or a "think-pair-share" activity to a student-created graphic organizer.

Guided Practice. Provide ample time for students to review what they have learned and to apply it with immediate feedback to identify inaccuracies. These applications can be oral or written, ranging from summarizing in graphic organizers, writing in journals, creating posters, and solving problems to teaching another student. All these activities will promote retention.

Closure. Have students summarize and apply what they have learned. This can be an oral or written activity done individually, with a partner or small group, or as a whole class. Unit closure activities can include delivering presentations, creating projects, performing skits, enacting simulations, role-playing events, or writing original songs.

Independent Practice. Have students review what they have learned to increase retention. Rehearsal is essential (Scarcella, 2003). Homework and practice are effective strategies to use to increase student achievement (Marzano, 2003). Homework policies must be made clear to parents, and students must know the purpose (Hill & Flynn, 2006). This practice is significant in making new learning a part of students' long-term knowledge and skills.

Step 5: Gather Resources and Supplementary Material

Identify textbook selections pertinent to your objectives. Then consider the needs of your students. You can record or have someone else record selections for review and reinforcement. Or you can adapt the text by rewriting complicated sections. You can choose other readings that complement the textbook selections.

Choose the audiovisual aids you will need to support your lesson or unit. Gather your props—from puppets to artifacts. Make the charts, graphs, and multimedia presentations you will need to provide background or illustrate significant points. Reserve the computer lab, if appropriate. List the materials for the science experiment. Pick out the manipulatives needed for the math activity. Flip the map holder to the correct map. Prepare graphic organizers, outlines, and study guides.

Step 6: Implement the Lesson

It's time to begin. Provide the graphic organizer(s), vocabulary support, and background information. Speak clearly and check for comprehension. Give students the opportunity to work with the problem or idea you present in small groups, or give them time to practice the new skill. Use the reading strategies mentioned in Chapter 5 to facilitate reading comprehension.

As you walk around to observe and listen to students working, describe what you see so the English learners have the chance to hear your speech and to connect their actions and the objects they handle to words. Watch for nonverbal reactions that show students are confused or are having difficulty understanding. When observing small groups, note if all group members are participating or not. Provide ample time for practice and remediation.

Step 7: Evaluation

At the conclusion of the unit, give students the opportunity to demonstrate that they have mastered the objectives. Whether the evaluation is a formal test or an alternative assessment, you will want to ask yourself the following questions: Were students successful? Could they demonstrate what they learned? Were they able to meet or exceed your expectations? What was surprising to you? What were the unanticipated obstacles and achievements? How did you feel about the lesson or unit? How was the pacing? What would you change if you were to do it again?

A LESSON PLAN FORMAT

With time, designing daily lessons will become automatic. In the meantime, having a plan to follow will facilitate your preparation. Table 9.1 offers a sample lesson plan format with reminders about how and where to make adaptations for your English learners.

Table 9.1   Sample Lesson Plan Format to Address English Learners

Lesson Plan Component	*Description and Suggestions for Adaptations for English Learner*
Title of Lesson	Brief description of content; relates to unit of study
Goal(s)	Broad statement of general knowledge, skills, and/or dispositions, usually aligned with state standards
Content Objective(s)	Specific statement of what students will know and be able to do in the subject area; includes new content, vocabulary, and skills
English Language Development Objective(s)	Specific statement of what students will be able to know and do with respect to standard English usage and grammar; includes vocabulary, terms, and grammar
Pre-Assessment	Tool to determine what students already know and are able to do; includes using pictures, gestures, building models as forms of response
Formative Assessment	Identifies progress monitoring for mastery of objectives; includes strategic questions for English learners and alternative assessments
Summative Assessment	Determines what evidence will be collected to show students have mastered objectives; includes adaptations, such as word banks and pictures, as well as alternatives for English learners
Anticipatory Set	Includes introductory activities to engage the learner; considers culture and experiences of English learners
Instructional Strategies and Student Activities	Describes what the teacher will do and what the students will do, as well as how they will be grouped and time allotted for each activity
Closure	Summarizes the learning; includes vocabulary, grammar, concepts, and skills
Practice	Includes in-class activities and homework to reinforce and apply the learning; can be guided and/or independent; considers experiences of English learners
Resources and Materials	Lists the items needed for successful implementation of lesson; includes advance organizers, vocabulary support, supplementary reading, and other materials, such as adapted texts, samples of student work, and rubrics for English learners
Evaluation	Reflection on the lesson after it is implemented; includes notes of progress on content area and English language development, difficulties encountered, and ideas on how to improve the lesson in the future

THE POWER OF LANGUAGE

This book was written to help you to both support your English learners while also challenging them to reach the high academic standards required of all students in public schools. As you do your best to support and challenge your students, you may well feel that you are engaged in a delicate balancing act. On one hand, you are doing your best to support the emotional, academic, and social needs of your students. On the other hand, you are required to challenge your students to meet rigorous academic standards and develop into capable and confident students. These tasks are not easy, but we hope that this book has provided you with the knowledge and tools needed to make this balancing act a bit easier.

Your classroom will be a unique place in which you will learn from your students and they will learn from you. You will have the opportunity to develop relationships with your students and to observe the progress they make while in your class. Over time, you will see your students master a new language as you improve your skills as a teacher. Perhaps the greatest gift you can ever offer to children, besides instilling a love of learning, is to help them express themselves in such a way that they are truly understood by others.

SUGGESTED ACTIVITIES

1. Incorporate the principles of brain research into one of your units. For example, chunk the material into meaningful segments, identify the appropriate metacognitive strategies you would have students implement, and plan time for reflection.

2. Consider the roles of emotion in learning, both as it relates to the classroom environment and as it applies to the readiness of individual learners to be successful.

3. Use the sample lesson plan format in this chapter to plan a series of lessons. Note the many adaptations for English learners.

4. Choose a variety of assessments from the list in this chapter to incorporate into a unit of study. Have students create rubrics to go along with the assessments.

5. Chart your students' progress. As English proficiency increases and gains in academic achievement are made, ask your students which strategies they feel were most helpful and why. Discuss how you can continue to support their success in the future.

References

2020 visions: Transforming education and training through advanced technologies. (n.d.). Retrieved February 26, 2007 from http://www.technology.gov/reports/TechPolicy/2020Visions.pdf.

Allen, R. (2000, Summer). Before it's too late: Giving reading a last chance. *Curriculum Update* (Association for Supervision and Curriculum Development), 1–8. Retrieved July 08, 2007 from http://www.ascd.org/video_demos/reading02/resources/reading1.html.

Allington, R. L., & Cunningham, P. M. (1996). *Schools that work: Where all children read and write.* New York: Longman.

Amanti, C. (1995). Teachers doing classroom research. *Practicing Anthropology, 17*(3), 7–9.

Andrews, R., Torgerson, C., Beverton, S., Freeman, A., Locke, T., Low, G., Robinson, A., & Zhu, D. (2006). The effect of grammar teaching on writing development. *British Educational Research Journal, 32*(1), 39–55.

Apple, M. (1979). On analyzing hegemony. *Journal of Curriculum Theorizing, 1*(1), 10–27.

Arends, R. (2004). *Learning to teach* (6th ed.). New York: McGraw Hill.

Atkinson, D. R., Morten, G., & Sue, D. W. (1997). *Counseling American minorities.* New York: McGraw-Hill.

Atwell, N. (1998). *In the middle: Writing, reading, and learning with adolescents.* Portsmouth, NH: Heineman.

Au, K. H. (1993). *Literacy instruction in multicultural settings.* New York: Harcourt Brace.

Bamberg, B. (1978). Composition instruction does make a difference: A comparison of the high school preparation of college freshmen in regular and remedial English classes. *Research in the Teaching of English, 12*, 47–59.

Bartholomew, B. (2007). Why we can't always get what we want. *Phi Delta Kappan, 88*(8), 593–598.

Berry, J. W., & Sam, D. L. (1997). Acculturation and adaptation. In J. Berry, M. Segall, & C. Kagitcibasi (Eds.), *Cross-cultural psychology* (pp. 291–326). Boston: Allyn & Bacon.

Bielenberg, B., & Wong-Fillmore, L. (December 2004/January 2005). The English they need for the test. *Educational Leadership, 62*(4), 45–49.

Boothe, D. (2000). Looking beyond the ESL label. *Principal Leadership, 1*(4), 30–35.

Bowen, J. D., Madsen, H., & Hilferty, A. (1985). *TESOL techniques and procedures.* Cambridge, MA: Newbury House.

Brown, A., & Palincsar, A. (1984). Reciprocal teaching of comprehension strategies: A natural history of one program for enhancing learning. *Technical Report No. 334.* Urbana: University of Illinois Center for the Study of Reading.

Burden, P. R. (2000). *Powerful classroom management strategies.* Thousand Oaks, CA: Corwin Press.

Cary, S. (2000). *Working with second language learners.* Portsmouth, NH: Heinemann.

Cassutto, G. (2000). Social studies and the World Wide Web. *International Journal of Social Education, 15*(1), 94–101.

Caulfield, J., Kidd, S., & Kocher, T. (2000). Brain-based instruction in action. *Educational Leadership, 58*(3), 62–65.

Chamot, A., & O'Malley, M. (1989). The Cognitive Academic Language Learning Approach. In P. Rigg & V. Allen (Eds.), *When they don't all speak English: Integrating the ESL student into the regular classroom* (pp. 108–125). Urbana, IL: National Council of Teachers of English.

Craig, M. (1994, April). *Students as ethnographers.* Paper presented at the meeting of the Society for Applied Anthropology, Cancun, Mexico.

Csikszentmihalyi, M. (1996). *Creativity: Flow and psychology of discovery and invention.* New York: HarperCollins.

Cummins, J. (1981). The role of primary language in promoting educational success for language minority students. In C. F. Leyba (Ed.), *Schooling and language minority students: A theoretical framework* (pp. 3–49). Los Angeles: Office of Bilingual Bicultural Education, California State University Evaluation, Dissemination, and Assessment Center.

Cummins, J. (1986). Empowering language minority students. *Harvard Educational Review, 15,* 18–36.

Cummins, J. (1996). *Negotiating identities: Education for empowerment in a diverse society.* Ontario, CA: California Association of Bilingual Education.

Curan, C. (1976). *Counseling learning in second language.* Apple River, IL: Apple River Press.

Daniels, H. (1994). *Literature circles: Voice and choice in the student-centered classroom.* Portland, ME: Stenhouse.

Daniels, H. (2002). *Literature circles: Voice and choice in book clubs and reading groups* (2nd ed.). Portland, ME: Stenhouse.

Davis, B. (2006). *How to teach students who don't look like you: Culturally relevant teaching strategies.* Thousand Oaks, CA: Corwin Press.

Delgado-Gaitan, C. (1993). Researching change and changing the researcher. *Harvard Educational Review, 63*(1), 389–411.

Delpit, L. (1995). *Other people's children.* New York: The New Press.

Deschler, D. (1983). *Kephart symposis.* Paper presented at Kephart Symposia, Aspen, CO.

Dhority, L., & Jensen, E. (1998). *Joyful fluency: Brain-compatible second language acquisition.* Thousand Oaks, CA: Corwin Press.

Dick, W., & Carey, L. (1990). *The systematic design of instruction.* New York: HarperCollins.

Echevarria, J., Vogt, M., & Short, D. J. (2004). *Making content comprehensible for English language learners: The SIOP model.* Boston: Pearson Allyn and Bacon.

Epstein, J. L., Sanders, M. G., Simon, B. S., Salinas, K. C., & Van Voohis, F. L. (2002). *School, family, and community partnerships: Your handbook for action* (2nd ed.). Thousand Oaks, CA: Corwin Press.

Faltis C. J., & Coulter, C. A. (2007). *English learners and immigrant teaching students in secondary schools.* Upper Saddle River, NJ: Prentice Hall.

Fisher, D., & Frey, N. (2003). Writing instruction for struggling adolescent readers: A gradual release model. *Journal of Adolescent & Adult Literacy 46*, 396–405.

Freeman, Y. S., & Freeman, D. E. (1998). *ESL/EFL teaching: Principles for success.* Portsmouth, NH: Heinemann.

Gallagher, K. (2006). *Teaching adolescent writers.* Portland, ME: Stenhouse.

Garcia, E. (1991). *The education of linguistically and culturally diverse students: Effective instructional practices (Educational Practice Report 1).* Santa Cruz, CA: National Center for Research on Cultural Diversity and Second Language Learning. Retrieved July 7, 2007 from http://www.ncela.gwu.edu/pubs/ncrcdsll/epr1/index.htm.

Gardner, H. (1983). *Frames of mind: A theory of multiple intelligences.* New York: Basic Books.

Gardner, H. (1999). *Intelligence reframed.* New York: Basic Books.

Gibbons, P. (2003). Mediating language learning: Teacher interactions with ESL students in a content-based classroom. *TESOL Quarterly, 37*(2), 247–273.

Gittings, J. (1995). Using household knowledge in special education. *Practicing Anthropology, 17*(3), 17–19.

Ginsberg, M. B. (2007). Lessons at the kitchen table. *Educational Leadership, 64*(6) 56–61.

Gonzalez, N. (1995). The Funds of Knowledge for Teaching Project. *Practicing Anthropology, 17*(3), 3–6.

Gray, T., & Fleischman, S. (December 2004/January 2005). Successful strategies for English language learners. *Educational Leadership, 62*(4), 84–85.

Grisham, D. (1999). Literacy partners: Supporting literacy innovation in a teacher study group. *Journal of Reading Education, 2,* 1–8.

Hairston, M. C. (1986). *Successful writing* (2nd ed.). New York: W. W. Norton.

Harper, C., & de Jong, E. (2004). Misconceptions about teaching English-language learners. *Journal of Adolescent & Adult Literacy, 48*(2), 152–162.

Harris, J. (1998). *Virtual architecture: Designing and directing curriculum-based telecomputing.* Eugene, OR: International Society for Technology in Education (ISTE).

Hazler, R. J. (1998). *Helping in the hallways: Advanced strategies for enhancing school relationships.* Thousand Oaks, CA: Corwin Press.

Heath, S. B. (1993). *Ways with words.* Cambridge, UK: Cambridge University Press.

Hensley, M. (1995). From untapped potential to creative realization: Empowering parents. *Practicing Anthropology, 17*(3), 13–16.

Herrell, A. (2000). *Fifty strategies for teaching English language learners.* Upper Saddle River, NJ: Merrill.

Hill, J. D., & Flynn, K. M. (2006). *Classroom instruction that works with English language learners.* Alexandria, VA: Association for Supervision and Curriculum Development.

Houk, F. A. (2005). *Supporting English language learners: A guide for teachers and administrators.* Portsmouth, NH: Heinemann.

Hunter, M. (1982). *Mastery teaching.* El Segundo, CA: T.I.P. Publications.

Jensen, E. (1995). *Super teaching.* Thousand Oaks, CA: Corwin Press.

Jesness, J. (2004). *Teaching English language learners K–12: A quick-start guide for the new teacher.* Thousand Oaks, CA: Corwin Press.

Johnson, D., & Johnson, R. (1998). *Learning together and alone* (5th ed.). Englewood Cliffs, NJ: Prentice Hall.

Kagan, S. (1994). *Cooperative learning.* San Juan Capistrano, CA: Kagan Cooperative Learning.

Kindler, A. L. (2002). *Survey of the states' limited English proficient students and available education programs and services. 2000–2001 Summary Report.* Washington, D.C.: National Clearinghouse for English Language Acquisition and Language Instruction Educational Programs.

Kottler, E., & Gallavan, N. P. (2008). *Secrets to success for social studies teachers.* Thousand Oaks, CA: Corwin Press.

Kottler, J. A. (2000). *Nuts and bolts of helping.* Boston: Allyn & Bacon.

Kottler, J. A., & Kottler, E. (2007). *Counseling skills for teachers.* Thousand Oaks, CA: Corwin Press.

Kottler, J. A., Zehm, S., & Kottler, E. (2005). *On being a teacher: The human dimension.* Thousand Oaks, CA: Corwin Press.

Krashen, S. (1984). *Writing: Research, theory, and applications.* New York: Pergamon Group.

Krashen, S. (1993). *The power of reading: Insights from the research.* Englewood, CO: Libraries Unlimited, Inc.

Krashen, S. (1996). *The natural approach: Language acquisition in the classroom* (Rev. ed.). Englewood Cliffs, NJ: Prentice Hall.

Krashen, S. (December 2004/January 2005). Skyrocketing scores: An urban legend. *Educational Leadership, 62*(4), 37–39.

Krashen, S., & Terrell, T. (1983). *The natural approach: Language acquisition in the classroom.* Englewood Clifts, NJ: Alemany Press.

Lachat, M. (2004). *Standards-based instruction and assessment for English language learners.* Thousand Oaks, CA: Corwin Press.

Lawrence, G., & Hunter, M. (1995). *Parent-teacher conferencing.* Thousand Oaks, CA: Corwin Press.

Lindemann, E. (1995). *A rhetoric for writing teachers.* New York: Oxford University Press.

Lindholm-Leary, K. (December 2004/January 2005). The rich promise of two-way immersion. *Educational Leadership, 62*(4), 56–59.

Lozanov, G. (1979). *Suggestology and outlines of suggestopedia.* New York: Gordon and Breach.

MacDonald, S. (1998). *The portfolio and its use: A roadmap for assessment.* Beltsville, MD: Gryphon House.

MacGillivray, L. (1995). Second language and literacy teachers considering literature circles: A play. *Journal of Adolescent and Adult Literacy, 39*(1), 36–44.

Manzo, A.V., Manzo, U. C., & Estes, T. H. (2001). *Content area literacy: Interactive teaching for active learning* (3rd ed.). New York: Wiley.

Marzano, R. J. (2003). *What works in schools: Translating research into action.* Alexandria, VA: Association for Supervision and Curriculum Development.

Mawhinney, T. S., & Sagan, L. L. (2007). The power of personal relationships. *Phi Delta Kappan, 88*(6), 460–464

Mayher, J. (1970). Linguistics for English teachers: What, why, and how they should know about language. Unpublished dissertation, Harvard Graduate School of Education.

Mayher, J. (1990). *Uncommon sense.* Portsmouth, NH: Heinemann.

Moje, E. B. (1996). "I teach students, not subjects": Teacher-student relationships as contexts for secondary literacy. *Research Reading Quarterly, 31*(2), 172–195.

Moll, L. C., Amanti, C., Neff, D., & Gonzalez, N. (1992). Funds of knowledge for teaching: Using a qualitative approach to connect homes and classrooms. *Theory Into Practice, 31*(2), 132–141.

Montgomery, M. (1999). *Building bridges with parents.* Thousand Oaks, CA: Corwin Press.

Muir-Herzig, R. (2004). Technology and its impact in the classroom. *Computers and Education, 42,* 111–131.

National Center for Education Statistics. (2005). *The condition of education 2005.* Washington, D.C.: U.S. Department of Education, Office of Educational Research and Improvement. Retrieved February 1, 2007 from http://nces.ed.gov/programs/quarterly/vol_7/1_2/9_1.asp.

National Institute of Child Health and Human Development. (2000). *Report of the National Reading Panel. Teaching children to read: An evidence-based assessment of the scientific research literature on reading and its implications for reading instruction: Reports of the subgroups* (NIH Publication No. 00–4754). Washington, D.C.: U.S. Government Printing Office.

Nieto, S. (Ed.). (2000). *Puerto Rican students in U.S. schools.* Mahwah, NJ: Lawrence Erlbaum Associates.

Nieto, S. (2002). *Language, culture, and teaching: Critical perspectives for a new century.* Mahwah, NJ: Lawrence Erlbaum Associates.

Nieto, S. (5th ed. 2008; 4th ed. 2004; 3rd ed., 2000; 2ne ed., 1996, 1st ed., 1992). *Affirming diversity: The sociopolitical context of multicultural education.* Boston: Allyn & Bacon Publishers, 4th & 5th eds.; New York: Longman Publishers, 1st through 3rd eds.

No Child Left Behind Act of 2001. (2001). 107th Congress of the United States of America. Retrieved February 1, 2007 from http://www.ed.gov/legislation/ESEA02/107–110.pdf.

Nunan, D. (1999). *Second language teaching and learning.* Boston: Heinle & Heinle.

Nurss, J. R., & Hough, R. A. (1992). Reading and the ESL student. In S. J. Samuels & A. E. Farstrup (Eds.), *What research has to say about reading instruction* (pp. 277–307). Newark, DE: International Reading Association.

Office of English Language Acquisition, Language Enhancement, and Academic Achievement for Limited English Proficient Students. (2002a). Retrieved July 9, 2007, from http://www.ncela.gwu.edu/policy/states/reports/statedata/2001/pdffiles/Iowa-Comp.pdf.

Office of English Language Acquisition, Language Enhancement, and Academic Achievement for Limited English Proficient Students. (2002b). Retrieved July 9, 2007, from http://www.ncela.gwu.edu/policy/states/reports/statedata/2001/pdffiles/Kansas-Comp.pdf.

Ogle, D. (1989). The know, want to know, learn strategy. In K. D. Muth (Ed.), *Children's comprehension of text: Research into practice* (pp. 205–233). Newark, DE: International Reading Association.

Olson, L. (2001). Test debate: What counts as multiple? *Education Week, 1*, 18–19.

Patterson, J. C. (2000, December). A handheld primer. *Curriculum Administrator's Education in Hand*, 4–8.

Pike, K., Compain, R., & Mumper, J. (1997). *New connections: An integrated approach to literacy*. New York: Addison-Wesley.

Pollock, J. (2007). *Improving student learning one teacher at a time.* Alexandria, VA: Association for Supervision and Curriculum Development.

Reksten, L. E. (2000). *Using technology to increase student learning.* Thousand Oaks, CA: Corwin Press.

Reiss, J. (2001). *ESOL Strategies for teaching content: Facilitating instruction for English language learners.* Upper Saddle River, NJ: Merrill Prentice Hall.

Reiss, J. (2008). *102 content strategies for English language learners: Teaching for academic success in grades 3–12.* Upper Saddle River, NJ: Merrill Prentice Hall.

Robins, K. N., Lindsey, R. B., Lindsey, D. B., & Terrell, R. D. (2002). *Culturally proficient instruction: A guide for people who teach.* Thousand Oaks, CA: Corwin Press.

Robinson, F. P. (1970). *Effective study* (4th ed.). New York: Harper & Row.

Robinson, T. L., & Howard-Hamilton, M. F. (2000). *The convergence of race, ethnicity, and gender.* Columbus, OH: Merrill.

Rumelhart, D. E. (1980). Schemata: The building blocks of cognition. In R. J. Spiro, B. C. Bruce, & W. F. Brewer (Eds.), *Theoretical issues in reading comprehension: Perspectives from cognitive psychology, linguistics, artificial intelligence, and education.* Hillsdale, NJ: Erlbaum.

Ryan, K., & Cooper, J. M. (2007). *Those who can, teach.* (11th ed.). New York: Houghton Mifflin.

Ryder, R., & Graves, M. (1998). *Reading and learning in content areas* (2nd ed.). Upper Saddle River, NJ: Prentice-Hall.

Ryder, R., & Graves, M. (2002). *Reading and learning in content areas* (3rd ed.). Hoboken, NJ: Wiley.

Sadker, D., Sadker, M., & Zittleman, K. (2008). *Teachers, schools, and society* (8th ed). New York: McGraw Hill.

Samway, K. D., & McKeon, D. (1999). *Myths and realities: Best practices for language minority students.* Portsmouth, NJ: Heinemann.

Santa, C. M., Havens, L. T., & Maycumber, E. M. (1996). *Project CRISS: Creating independence through student-owned strategies.* Dubuque, IA: Kendall/Hunt.

Scarcella, R. (1990). *Teaching language minority students in the multicultural classroom.* Englewood Cliffs, NJ: Prentice Hall Regents.

Scarcella, R. (2003). *Accelerating academic English: A focus on English language learners.* Oakland, CA: Regents of the University of California.

Schrock, K. (2002). The ABC's of Web site evaluation. Retrieved January 16, 2007 from http://school.discovery.com/schrockguide/pdf/weval.pdf.

Schurr, S. (1999). *Authentic assessment: Using product, performance, and portfolio measures from A to Z.* Westerville, OH: National Middle School Association.

Seely, C., & Romijn, E. (1995). *TPR is more than commands: At all levels.* Berkeley, CA: Command Performance Language Institute.

Sharan, Y., & Sharan, S. (1992). *Expanding cooperative learning through group investigation.* New York: Teachers College Press.

Short, D., & Echevarria, J. (December 2004/January 2005).Teacher skills to support English language learners. *Educational Leadership, 62*(4), 8–13.

Slavin, R. (1988). *Student team learning: An overview and practical guide.* Washington, D.C.: National Education Association.

Sousa, D. (2004). *How the brain learns* (3rd ed.). Thousand Oaks, CA: Corwin Press.

Stock, P. L. (1995). *The dialogic curriculum: Teaching and learning in a multicultural society.* Portsmouth, NH: Heinemann.

Street, C. (Fall/Winter 2000). Using word-processing software to improve the writing attitudes of reluctant writers. *English in Texas, 30*(2), 35–37.

Street, C. (2002). The P.O.W.E.R. of process writing in content area classrooms. *Journal of Content Area Reading, 1*(1), 43–54.

Street, C. (2003). Pre-service teachers' attitudes about writing and learning to teach writing: Implications for teacher educators. *Teacher Education Quarterly, 30*(3), 33–50.

Street, C. (2005a). Funds of knowledge at work in the writing classroom. *Multicultural Education, 13*(12), 22–25.

Street, C. (2005b). A reluctant writer's entry into a community of writers. *Journal of Adolescent & Adult Literacy, 48*(8), 636–641.

Street, C. (2005c). Using the Internet to explore the French revolution. *The Social Studies, 96*(1), 41–42.

Thomas, W. P., & Collier, V. (1997). *School effectiveness for language minority students.* Washington, D.C.: National Clearinghouse for Bilingual Education.

Timm, J. (1996). *Four perspectives in multicultural education.* New York: Wadsworth.

Tomlinson, C. A. (2003). Deciding to teach them all. *Educational Leadership, (61)*2, 6–11.

Tomlinson, C. A., & McTighe, J. (2006). *Integrating differentiated instruction and understanding by design: Connecting content and kids.* Alexandria, VA: Association for Supervision and Curriculum Development.

U.S. Census Bureau. (August, 2000). *Census brief: Coming to America.* Retrieved January 29, 2007, from http://www.census.gov/prod/2000pubs/cenbr002.pdf.

U.S. Department of Education. (2003). *Paige outlines No Child Left Behind Act's "Ten key benefits for parents of English language learners."* Retrieved January 29, 2007, from http://www.ed.gov/news/pressre leases/2003/12/12022003.html

U.S. Immigration and Naturalization Service. (1999). *Office of policy and planning statistics branch annual report* (No. 2). Washington, DC: Author.

Vargas-Reighley, R. (2005). *Bi-cultural competence and academic resilience among immigrants.* New York: LFB Scholarly Publishing LLC.

Velez-Ibanez, C. G. (1996). *Border visions.* Tucson: The University of Arizona Press.

Villegas, A. M., & Lucas, T. (2007). The culturally responsive teacher. *Educational Leadership, 64*(6), 28–33.

Wiggins, G., & McTighe, J. (2005). *Understanding by design* (expanded 2nd ed.). Upper Saddle River, NJ: Pearson Education, Inc.

Wilhelm, J. (2004). Inquiring minds use technology. *Voices from the Middle, 11*(3), 45–47.

Wolfe, P. (2001). *Brain matters: Translating research into classroom practice.* Alexandria, VA: Association for Supervision and Curriculum Development.

Wolk, S. (2003). Hearts and minds. *Educational Leadership, 61*(1), 14–18.

Zinsser, W. (2006). *On writing well* (30th anniversary edition). New York: HarperCollins.

Zwiers, J. (2004). *Developing academic thinking skills in grades 6–12: A handbook of multiple intelligence activities.* Newark, DE: International Reading Association.

Index

CORWIN PRESS

The Corwin Press logo—a raven striding across an open book—represents the union of courage and learning. Corwin Press is committed to improving education for all learners by publishing books and other professional development resources for those serving the field of PreK–12 education. By providing practical, hands-on materials, Corwin Press continues to carry out the promise of its motto: **"Helping Educators Do Their Work Better."**